"I've Always Wanted to Run a Bed and Breakfast!"

THE SECRETS TO STARTING
&
RUNNING A SUCCESSFUL B&B

by

Chris and Michelle Bengivengo

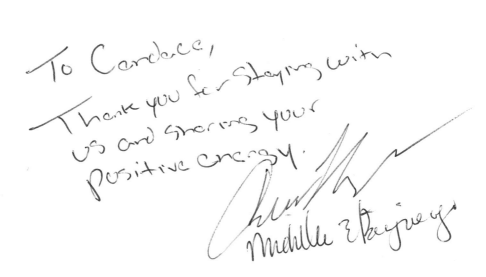

To Candace,
Thank you for staying with us and sharing your positive energy.

Chris
Michelle E Bengivengo

ISBN: 1-4392-0315-6
ISBN-13: 9781439203156

Visit www.booksurge.com to order additional copies.

DEDICATION

For Amy

Thank you for sharing the joys of your life
and providing me with the motivation to write this book.

CONTENTS

"I've Always Wanted to Run a Bed and Breakfast!"

PREFACE

This is the story of how we came to live our dream of running a bed and breakfast and the many important lessons we learned along the way. We will freely share the details of how to start and run a bed and breakfast, along with some personal insights we have gained through our experience as innkeepers.

Reading this book, we hope you will be inspired to follow your own dreams whatever they may be, and accept as truth that life does have a plan for you if you will only trust in the universe to provide you all that you need, and seek to live a life less for the future, and more in the moment.

It was a great personal awakening when I realized that I have everything right now that I need to do what is next in my life. It is a cop out to say "if only I had" or "when I get ..." that you will follow your dreams. Follow them now, and follow them with confidence.

We truly hope you find success on your journey of discovery, whether you are looking to start a bed and breakfast of your own, or you simply desire to make some changes in your way of thinking that will place you on the higher path in life you were destined to walk.

FOREWORD

JUST JUMP!

We are all brought up with the notion that if you work hard all your life, at some point you will receive a gold watch and a pension to carry you through a happy and restful future. The problem with this fairy tale is that when you are actually participating in the process, you find that there are never any guarantees.

My story is not unique. I started out at 18 moving out on my own, doing a hitch in the service, attending college, becoming trained as a Firefighter/

Paramedic, and then employment in the emergency services field. I liked what I was doing, worked hard, and managed to obtain the rank of Assistant Fire Chief before "retiring."

The problem was, that after twenty-five years of toil and effort I had not earned the pension I envisioned, and my measure of success was trampled because I had failed to make Fire Chief, my ultimate working goal. The reasons for this rival those of so many similarly disillusioned stories, perhaps even yours. Backstabbing coworkers, inept bosses, bad timing and politics all had a hand in my reaching my late forties and still not obtaining my goals.

Is it a coincidence that this frustrated feeling came on just as I was looking at my fifties?

I have spent many hours considering the mid-life crisis possibility. The outcome of this deep analyzing of my life was a belief that it was something more, a calling, a kick in the butt from some higher source that was tempting me from the life I had built to the life I was destined to live.

It took a lot of courage to leave my career in the fire service and to embark on a path that was so unclear. I was accustomed to the comfort of a secure paycheck, wonderful benefits, and a feeling that the future was going to be taken care of. Basically, living my now for some future benefit. Ultimately, however, it became clear that the present is where I needed to focus my attention.

Part of the gold-watch philosophy is that the future is where the payoff is, and today is just a place you toil to get there. Sure, there are milestones in life that bring us to a more immediate focus; our first sexual experience, graduating high school and again from college, getting married, having children, perhaps even the death of a parent. If you think about it, it is these focus moments in our lives, the ones where we are fully in the moment, that become the memories we hold most dear. It also strikes me funny that when someone has a close brush with death and later describes seeing their life pass before their eyes, the scenes they describe are comprised of these moments.

A female friend of mine who is a high-level professional in a career that requires her to be on call 24-hours a day has a sign on her desk that says it all. It reads, "No one on their death bed ever said, I wish I had worked more."

For me, the scary part of making the initial leap from my pre-programmed future reward- based existence to the one I was destined for, was not feeling in control of what my new life would turn out to be. Yes, I had big ideas, but if my all-or-nothing move was going to be successful, I had to have an open mind to allow my new life to unfold as the universe intended. This letting go of control was, and still is, very difficult for me.

A great help to me was my wife Michelle, an angelic soul with a heart of gold, and a natural present-moment liver. Her support and love are a constant comfort to me and with her I am left wanting nothing more in my life. Recognizing my struggle to move from a future-based life to a present moment existence, she would often encourage me by saying, "Just pick up your feet and let the current of the universe take you to where you need to be." then she would soften into a loving smile and conclude, "Remember, you can't screw it up." a liberating philosophy I would soon come to trust.

In truth, I had no choice in the matter of leaving my chosen career and venturing out into the world of living in the moment and trusting the universe to provide. I realized this when I found myself chronically arriving late to the office. I then found myself searching for the fortitude not to leave early, all the day robotically accomplishing the reoccurring tasks associated with my position. I hated the routine of my life, even though I believed in the importance of my job.

I knew it was time to leave when the day arrived that I could simply no longer pick myself up out of bed and drag my body, mind, and spirit into the office for even one more day. The life I had so diligently built was killing me, not just spiritually, but also physically, and I had proof sitting right on my bedside table.

So, how many medications are you on? Do you have mild to moderate high blood pressure, or a borderline diabetic problem? How about an enlarged prostate or cervical issues? Do you listen to and believe the "You can't live without our pill!" bedtime story you see on TV every night? The commercials are everywhere, especially in the evening when the pharmaceutical companies know you are watching, all showing powerful imagery of how perfect our lives would be if you would simply take their pills. I was not even in my mid-forties when I became entranced by this bedtime story. I was taking pills for blood pressure, prostate, and cholesterol, all of which thankfully, under a Doctor's supervision, I am off of today. Why? Because I now actively approach life in a way that does not allow the root of all disease, Distress, to be the master of my life.

We all experience stress, as it is an inevitable part of life. There are two types of stress, Eustress, or good stress, and Distress, the bad stuff. Eustress is the stress that motivates you to complete the necessary tasks in life. For example, eustress is the spark that causes us to care for our newborn children. These newly arrived bundles of joy require almost constant attention and care, and when they have any need at all that is unmet, they do what they do best, cry! The parenting task fully tests our patience and is fraught with challenges, but the overshadowing joy we experience makes it all worthwhile and is ultimately good for our physical and spiritual development.

Distress is the opposite. Although many of the same physiologic effects take place in the body as with eustress, many more bad ones occur when experiencing distress including, constriction of the peripheral veins resulting in a rise in blood pressure, an over- production of stomach acid causing ulcers, shallow breathing leading to fatigue, and tensing of muscles causing migraines and joint problems. When these natural responses to a threat that are genetically programmed to ensure our physical survival, such as when a woolly mammoth enters the family cave intending to have you for dinner, become chronically turned on, our bodies pay the price of "dis-ease" ultimately resulting in a premature death. Your Doctor will surely agree that anything you can do to reduce the distress in your life will be good for you and will add years to your life.

As we live and have successful and unsuccessful life experiences, we gain wisdom. Have you ever heard a son say of his dad; "I used to think my father's advice was stupid, until I got older?" So perhaps it takes until midlife for us to learn to trust ourselves enough to start making choices based upon what is good for us physically and what brings positive personal growth and peace of mind, even if it is a life that is contrary to the fairy tale of the gold watch.

I did it. I took that scary leap into the unknown, and it has been one of the best things I have ever done. You can do it too. Remember, you can't screw it up!

INTRODUCTION

Being an Innkeeper can be a fun and rewarding experience if you are prepared. Like any other career you may consider, it pays to do your research and understand the ins and outs of the business and what it takes to be a success. The best way to do this is to talk with folks who are doing now what you are considering, and get some direct insight into what their daily lives are like. Sometimes what we imagine to be perfect turns out in reality to be something else. If you doubt me, just ask anyone who is divorced. A cheap joke, I know, but there is truth in the fact that once you have had an experience, i.e. running a certain type of business, you can share the knowledge you have gained with others headed down the same path, and hopefully help them avoid the same mistakes you made. So, let's talk.

I call running a B&B a business, but really it is a lifestyle. Lifestyle careers are those that require more than a nine to five commitment. In fact, as the label "lifestyle" implies, running a B&B is a way of life, one that requires a commitment of time and energy that is all-consuming and may come as shock for those who are unprepared. It is hoped that this guide will help potential Innkeepers understand the business they are considering and what it takes to be successful.

When Michelle and I started our B&B we knew little of what it took to do so. We were both in careers like many of you, that involved working for someone else and guided by our employer's goals and desires. If they wanted us to work weekends we had little choice. If our boss was a jerk, there was little we could do. We were slaves to our paychecks and the needs of others. Michelle and I wanted more control of our lives and to be more fulfilled by our toil. We wanted the rewards of our hard work and energy to be in our hands, not our bosses'. This I'm sure, is a common motivation to go into business for yourself, and we were no different.

Along the way from being corporate, or in our case, municipal slaves, to being self-employed, in our case as Innkeepers, much had to be learned and we will try to share some of this newfound knowledge with you here. Michelle and I both have Public Education backgrounds and were paid by our employers to teach others in a fun and inviting way to understand new processes and procedures unfamiliar to them. With this book, we will attempt to provide you with insight into the lifestyle of innkeeping while exposing the pitfalls and joys that come along with starting and running a bed and breakfast. Each section covers a specific area of consideration, planning, and operation for the potential B&B owner, along with tips that we hope will help you succeed.

When reading this guide, keep a pen and paper nearby to jot down notes of the points that are important to you. If you follow the exercises we suggest, and are honest with yourself, when you are done reading this book you should have a clear feeling if being an innkeeper is right for you, and a roadmap for establishing and operating a successful B&B of the size, in a location, and offering the services, that are right for you. Now lets get started!

CHAPTER 1

Your Goals and Desires List

Ugh! A goals and desires list, what am I twelve?

What ever you do don't pass up this step! I know it seems that creating a goals and desires list is an elementary exercise that most of us have not done since our high school career counselors made us make one years ago, but a G&D list is very useful when making any major change in your life. It helps you to clarify your expectations of what you want the results of your efforts to be. Not only will it help you decide if being a B&B owner is right for you, but it will help aim you in the direction you need to go in life to get all the rewards you desire.

Before we make your list let's talk about Manifesting. Manifesting is a process by where you visualize your goals and desires and live your life as if they already exist. This in turn will make them a reality. In today's world you hear more and more about the power of manifesting your own reality. New Age authors will tell you that manifesting is a powerful tool and a true force in nature that cannot be ignored, like gravity, and if properly exercised can create untold wealth and happiness in your life. Whether or not you believe in manifesting is up to you, but I suggest that there is no harm in the process.

One caution. Many folks who start the process of manifesting their own reality get discouraged because they do not get the results they desire as quickly as they like. This is by design. Think about it. If you truly got everything you wanted when you thought you wanted it, what other fantastic experiences or encounters would you have missed out on that later proved to be more beneficial in your life? The Universe has a way of knowing what challenges and lessons you need to grow as a unique person, and it will always provide you the proper tools and circumstances whether you think they are right for you at the time or not.

Just remember, you have all the skills, knowledge, wealth, and ability to do what is required next in your life, right now! Do not say, "as soon as I get whatever paid off", or "as soon as the kids are…" or "when I'm older I will…" Thinking that the desire you feel pushing you in a new direction cannot be satisfied at the current time due to some influence that you don't control is flawed and makes STRESS, and bad stress that you want to avoid. To borrow a slogan, "Just Do It!" There are numerous books on the subject of manifesting your own reality and I suggest you seek out one or two and read up on how the process truly works; now onto making your list.

Do not make your G&D list a complicated task. Just sit down with a pencil and paper and list your goals in order of importance. If you are thinking of opening a B&B with your life partner, you both should make an individual list first. Let the other person do this task in his or her own way. The goal is to have an honest list of each person's individual priorities and desires. After each of you is done, you should find a relaxing spot and read your lists to each other, sharing your priorities. This can be a very enlightening process that will show if opening a bed and breakfast together is going to meet each other's expectations.

Here is an example of the first five things on Chris' list:

1. Work with Michelle
2. Give me time to myself
3. Generate an income equal to my current salary including benefits
4. Time to write
5. Be a source of positive inspiration to others

Michelle and I had talked for years about how much we hated being apart from each other for even a short time. We worked together for the same employer and worked closely together, we lived together, and we had all the same friends. Whenever we were apart, we would feel at a loss and if someone we knew saw us alone, they would ask where the other was. For the quality of my life, doing something where we could always be near to each other was the highest priority.

Note: Being in business with, and working so closely with your spouse is something that should be examined very closely by both of you. Can you do it?

The next thing on my list stems from what was most nagging me at the time Michelle and I were considering opening a business together. My present job was very intrusive into my time. I had to be available at all hours of the day and night. When I did manage to get some time off, inevitably something would occur where I was made to feel guilty that I could not be reached. I desperately felt that I needed to gain more control of my own time or I would surely be dead from a heart attack before I was fifty.

The third item on my list represented a satisfaction with the income level I had obtained working for others and my desire to maintain our standard of living.

Fourth on the list was time to write. I love writing and have many completed and incomplete stories on my computer. I know you may say that if I am a writer I would make time no matter what, but I challenge you that what I am really talking about here is making a life where I feel at ease in taking time to write.

Fifth, Michelle and I have always lived in a manner that we look for the meaning and lessons in life. We always seek to have the things we do be properly motivated and live our lives in a giving way. Doing so, we have met many wonderful people and have had countless positive experiences that have helped us to grow.

Here is an example of the first five things on Michelle's list:

1. Something we can do together.
2. Generates enough wealth to enjoy life.
3. Contributes to my spiritual growth.
4. Gives me time to pursue personal interests.
5. Allows me to wear what that I want.

Ah! You see we were instinctively together on our desire to work with each other. To be completely honest, we had discussed the possibility so much; we knew it was a mutual priority.

Number 2 again shows our agreement that the standard of living we had was the one we wanted to maintain.

Knowing Michelle, I know that number 3 could have been number 1 on her list. I am sure that I heavily influenced her by my speaking about it, items 1 and 2 on her list. I love that she listens to me and made my priorities hers. Michelle looks at the world in a way that she sees the beauty and awe of life first, and she usually leaves the cynicism to me. She is a Yogi and just being around her you can tell. Having how she lives her life not contribute to her spiritual growth is impossible.

Michelle too was feeling that her time was not her own and found it very frustrating that the things that were important to her personally were always coming last. After her Yoga interest took off, this became more and more of a drag on her outlook. To be at peace, she needed to take time to be in her own world and get away from the one imposed by others.

This last item may have been farther down on her list but I include it to provide an example of the type of things you should consider about what you hope to achieve. I sometimes jokingly call Michelle "Earth Girl" as she had what I call "hippie" tendencies. She dresses comfortably in earthy clothes, recycles religiously, like me is a vegetarian, and her favorite car was her VW Bug. Working for a municipal fire department as an educator, she was required to wear a uniform, including restrictions on how she wore her hair. A bug in her bonnet was the promotion-seeking, mid-level fire officers who would constantly bug her to modify the way she wore her brass pin insignias and nameplate, or to put up her hair, or polish her shoes. None of these things were important to her. She was comfortable being herself. Rules about hair length or sock color were, to Michelle, for firefighters, not teachers. To be able to wear her earthy clothes and to let her hair down (and she has a lot of it) were things that made her who she was. Wearing a uniform was not.

These are just examples of the beginning of our lists, as there were many more things we each wrote down. Your list should be as long as necessary to cover the things that are important to you, but try to keep it between ten and twenty items. Remember to put the highest priority items first. These should be the things you will not compromise in your visualization of the future. You can also indicate nice-to-have things as you go, but be clear on the separation.

If you are working with a spouse or partner, you will need to compare your lists and see where they overlap, and even more importantly, where they don't. Try to generate a combined list that you are both content with. Be honest! This is the foundation for the future. If you cheat here, you may be very disappointed later. Once you are done, keep your priority list handy as you read the rest of this book. It is your yardstick and it will help you measure if being an innkeeper is right for you and will allow you to obtain your goals.

CHAPTER 2

Is a B&B the right business for you?

I know, why would you be reading a book on starting a B&B if you did not think it was right for you? Well, let's see how you feel after completing our next exercise. Now take out your G&D list that you completed in chapter one. Next take out the local phone book and open it to the yellow pages. Now take a fresh pencil and paper and starting with the A's, using your G&D list as a guide, look at each type of business and consider if it would be possible to meet the things on your list if you owned each type of business.

For example could you meet your goals and desires by being a barber? Let's try this with Chris' list from chapter one.

1. Work with Michelle - No. (Unless she wants to be a barber too)
2. Give me time to myself - Probably not as I may have to be open long hours and weekends.
3. Salary equal to my current pay- Doubtful unless I have others working for me.
4. Time to write - No
5. Positive inspiration to others - Yes (I can be a positive example in anything I do)

So being a barber looks doubtful to fulfill my goals and desires.

Keep going and do this exercise for any business that you think may match your list. You can skip things that you know you would not consider because of the new education required, like a physician or engineer, or that you might find too creepy, like being a mortician. But do the exercise for any business that is possible.

Michelle and I considered numerous businesses before choosing to run a B&B. We looked at coffee shops, ice cream stores, gift shops, yoga studios, convenience stores, boat rental services, sail charter services, consulting, and tool rental services.

After you complete the phone book exercise, look at the businesses that potentially fit your G&D list. Now go back and find one or two that are nearby and go visit them. This does not mean you have to go in and announce that you are thinking of opening a business just like theirs. You can, in the case of an ice cream shop for example, visit as a customer, but use your eyes like an owner. What is involved in running the business? Is the owner running things or is a hired clerk? What are the operating hours listed on the door? Does the work involved look like something you want to do? Consider the time the business is not open to the public that prep work, or receiving deliveries is required. How many permits and licenses are posted?

All of these things give you clues to the true work involved in operating the type of business, and you can see if it feels right to you in observation. If it does, you may consider chatting with the owner. Explain that you are considering opening such a business, but not in competition with them (be honest about this). Ask them if they would share with you some insights and if they are happy. Most successful business owners are more than happy to brag about their success and have the confidence to share their knowledge without fear that doing so will hurt them. If the owner is leery talking with you, there may be a reason. Who knows, during your discussions, you may even find an owner who is ready to sell!

> *Michelle's Thought: Consider the amount of physical exertion you'll be doing. If you've got tricky knees or a bad back, you might be challenged by all the lifting and carrying heavy loads, going up and down many flights of stairs a day, or by moving furniture or mattresses and bedsprings around. All are things that we do repeatedly.*

Complete this process for as many businesses you are considering, use your G&D list all the while. If you are going to be working with a spouse or partner, make these visits together. You each have to decide the type of business that is right for you.

You should take as long in researching potential business as you can comfortably afford, or until you eliminate all but one business type from your list. In our case, Michelle and I had a ninety-day period where I was not working and she had control over her yoga-teaching schedule enough to allow us to really explore our potential businesses. We visited numerous businesses in our area, and even contacted business brokers to look at some more closely and get a handle on the financials. This part is like buying a house; you learn what you truly want by looking at numerous listings inside and out. Then you get a broker, secure financing if necessary, and see if you can get it for a fair price.

I cannot stress the importance of the method of looking for a business similar to the one you are considering that is for sale and pursuing it as if you were going to buy it. You will have access to very detailed operation and financial information that you otherwise would not. If you are astute, you will be able to rapidly assess if the standard of living a particular type of business provides is one that matches your Goals and Desires list.

Keep in mind that business owners are as diverse as coworkers at the office. Some will be good at what they do and some will not. By visiting a few different business of each type you will be able to tell the general time commitment required, level of income produced, and work necessary to operate it. Some of this is in the gut. In fact, I caution that even if a business looks like it can meet all the items on your G&D list, if your gut (or your partner's) is telling you it is not right, move on to something else.

Remember "the grass is always greener" syndrome. You may be excited and ready to own your own business, but if you are not careful, you may not see the pitfalls that are plain to others. To help avoid this, I suggest that once you narrow things down to the type of business you want to own, talk with a trusted friend or family member who you know will be honest with you. Ask them what they see right, and more importantly, wrong with your plan. Take notes and don't be defensive. It is just objective information for you to consider. You ultimately get to decide what you do with your life, not them, and if they truly have your best interests in mind, they will support you no matter what you do.

CHAPTER 3

So you've decided to open a Bed and Breakfast

Now that you have decided that running a B&B is the business for you, let's talk a bit about the lifestyle. You live a B&B. Not only do you live in your business, the interference in your daily life is constant. I am not trying to discourage you here, just give you a reality check as to what you are getting into.

I can not tell you how many folks that stay at our B&B say; "I have always wanted to do this", and on the surface it does look like a fun way to make a living. When we get talking with them however, most realize that their personality is not exactly right for the job. If you are opening a B&B with your partner, their personality is also important.

A very close friend of ours who had run a successful business of her own for many years was considering moving south and opening a B&B in a tourist town. After staying with us a few times while we had guests, she began to question her ability to do so. It had nothing to do with her skills in running a business; after all she was already a successful business owner. Her concern was her honest knowledge that she had trouble with people being too much in her personal space. She knew that it made her very nervous and even grumpy when she wanted her privacy and others required her time.

I encourage this same type of honest assessment on your part, How are you going to react when you are just sitting down to watch your favorite TV show and the phone rings, or better yet, you get a drive-up (a guest without a reservation looking for a room)? Can you set aside your personal plans to accommodate your guest? How about canceling a weekend outing you had been planning for weeks at the last minute because you take a reservation? Can your personality adjust, and can you keep a smile on your face?

We will talk in detail about reservation policies and practices later but just a quick note here. There was a time when folks planned months, even a year in advance for their next vacation. Well no more. In today's fast paced, Blackberry, 70-hour workweek world, people get away when a break suddenly presents itself, and that is usually on very short notice. If you are lucky you will know a month in advance that a guest is planning to stay with you. More realistically it will be only a week or two.

If you have a business partner, you may be able to avoid some of these distractions through planning and unselfish support of one another. If groceries need to be bought, one of you can go to the store while the other waits for guest arrivals. It is important that both of you get some time away from your business, even if it is just for a haircut. What is trickier is getting away together, say for dinner or out for a movie. There will be plenty of nights where you have no guests and can do so, but you have to understand that your plans could change with a phone call. You have to roll with the punches and be grateful for the business. You have to take it when it comes. You may expect a holiday weekend to be busy and get no one then suddenly be full on a Wednesday.

Michelle's Thought: Chris and I both are lucky enough to label ourselves as "home-bodies"; we enjoy being in our home, being together, and also each of us have "home friendly" skills. Chris can fix just about ANYTHING that breaks, I enjoy gardening, sewing and baking; all pastimes that fit in nicely with running a bed & breakfast! Not everyone that runs a B&B needs to enjoy doing things and being at home, but it sure helps.

Consider this; There is nothing worse than when I go into a store or shop and for some reason the owner is distracted and makes me feel as if I am putting him or her out by being there. What is more important than a paying customer? What are these people in business for if not to meet their customer's needs and ultimately get my cash into their register? I am sure, if you think about it, you can recall many instances where you have felt the same way. Think back on your experience. Did you leave the shop feeling as if you would never return?

In the B&B business, guests equal dollars, and happy guests mean repeat business in the future, a very important part of running a B&B. I would say almost a third of our business is repeat guests, and we would not make a profit without them. In fact, we enjoy them, as they are familiar and comfortable with our Inn even before they arrive.

There have been times when Michelle and I expected a repeat guest on a night when we wanted to attend a family event like a school play. Having a prior relationship with these guests we were able to comfortably allow them to arrive and make themselves at home without us being there to personally greet them. We of course, either inform them in advance that this is what is going to occur, or we leave them a "Note from the Innkeepers" card that welcomes them and tells them where we are, when we expect to return, and a cell phone number to call if they need us. Use caution though, you should do this only with your most familiar guests who will not feel slighted by your absence.

Okay, so you think you can share your space and time with strangers with out losing it. This is a great start—every innkeeper I have talked to, including us, will tell you that the best part of being an innkeeper is the people you meet. Folks come from all over the world, are varied in age and background, and have exciting stories to share. You should always make the time to chat with your guests if they are amenable, at breakfast is a good time, as this is how you get to know them personally and build a relationship with them. Personal relationships are what bring your guests back time and time again.

Michelle is very good about this task. She always remembers our guest's names, the names of their children even if they are not with them, even the names of their pets. She keeps guest notes that detail what type of special requests they may have had. If a hair dryer was requested, we make sure one is in the room the next time the guest arrives, if they are allergic to certain foods or prefer their coffee black, she notes it. This way we can personalize their service on their next stay and they know we care about them being here.

Michelle's Thought: He's such a flatterer! True, I do try to get to know each and every one of our guests personally, and treat each one as special, because they are. I am an honest believer in the old adage, "People may not remember what you said or what you were wearing when you first met them, but they WILL remember how to MADE THEM FEEL." If you simply put yourself in your guests' shoes; what made you feel comfortable and at home last time YOU went somewhere? Ask everyone you know that has ever visited a B&B what they liked about their experience, and more importantly, what they didn't like. Don't be afraid to ask your guests, too. We are as open to suggestions, concerns, and "you know what might be nice?" comments as we are to compliments, and we encourage our guests to share accordingly.

So the question is; do you (and does your partner) have the personality to be an innkeeper? You will get all levels of demands from your guests, from those who want a discount on everything from the room to the breakfast, and all the extras you can provide, to those who you almost never see. Inn keeping is a customer service business. Past experience dealing directly with the public will be extremely helpful to you. At least one of you, you or your partner, should be good at this. Knowing how to control a situation while being gracious is a valuable skill that will be tested often.

CHAPTER 4

What type of B&B do you want?

Isn't a bed and breakfast just a bed and breakfast? If you have stayed at many B&B's you already know the answer. B&B's, and the services they offer, are as varied as the folks that run them. That is a great part of being a B&B owner. You can make your B&B just what you want it to be, and there is no one to tell you can't. It is not only your business, but also your house, and your inn will end up reflecting your personality and individuality just as your home does now. But first, we must get a clearer picture of what you want your B&B to be. Here are some things to consider. Better get that pen and paper again…

- Where do you want to live?
- What vintage house do you want?
- What theme do you want to present?
- How many guest rooms do you want?
- Do you want a staff?
- Do you want a restaurant?
- Do you want to do weddings and special events?
- Do you want a gift shop?
- How much property do you want to own?
- What kind of guests do you want to attract?

Write down your answers to these questions keeping them consistent with the vision of the B&B you see in your mind. At this point anything is possible, and your thoughts should not be modified based on practical matters like available cash or geography. Just have fun with your answers imagining the B&B of your dreams. When you are done, read on. This chapter will provide you with some practical considerations on each point that will help you fine-tune your picture.

Where do you want to live?

Fiji, The Carolinas, Vermont, Key West. Where you want to live is important to both your personal satisfaction with your geographic location, and the personality of your Inn. It would be something to want to live in Fiji but also want a 100-year-old New England style home. Who knows though, this may be just what you want– and that's okay too. The combination may make you unique in the market and generate fantastic business!

By this time in your life, I am sure you have a good idea where you want to live, at least for the next five or ten years. Perhaps you live in the northeast and want to move to Florida? Perhaps, as it was for Michelle and me, the opposite is true. You know if a warm climate is right for you, or do you prefer a cold one? You really should have some idea where you want to operate your B&B by now. Just make sure you understand that moving to the islands to open a B&B will present different challenges than if you open one in your hometown where you already know where to shop, the fun things to do, and have a support system of family and friends that can help you. Lastly, if you want to attract snow skiers, an inn in Key West is a stretch.

What vintage house do you want?

Michelle and I run an inn in a house that is over 100 years old; houses of this vintage present with great charm and warmth. The woodwork is abundant, including the original hardwood floors. The ceilings are high, the stairs wide and inviting. Every creak of the floor and whine of the pipes adds to our guests' experience and makes our inn seem alive and comforting. But, older houses can be a charm or a curse. Systems like plumbing and electric may be old and might require updating to meet code. This will add greatly to your start-up costs. The foundation may need reinforcing, the furnace could be inefficient, insulation may be lacking. On the other hand, newer houses are just not built like older ones. Large windows, open stairs, mudrooms, even basements are hard to find in new construction. And don't forget the large wrap-around porch, something new homebuilders have sacrificed for more interior square footage.

Newer properties have the advantage of more efficient heating and cooling systems, modern plumbing and electrical systems, newer appliances, and code compliant safety systems. Unless they are built in a vintage style, however, they usually do not have the charm of an older structure. This can be overcome with creative decorating, but again this adds to your start-up costs. The better approach is to let your house be what it is, new or old, and simply focus on making it expresses your personality in a way that is inviting to your guests. Not everyone cares if your house was built 15 or 150 years ago. They just want a nice place to stay.

What theme do you want to present?

Theme is important in a few ways. First, when on vacation, people usually want to experience the flavor of the location they are visiting. If you traveled to Nepal would you want to stay at a Holiday Inn? Or would you like to stay in a stone stacked mountain lodge with prayer flags flapping on lines strung outside? If your desire is to live in Key West you should probably tailor your theme to the ambiance and feel of the tropics, and the nautical history of the island. You do not have to go overboard on this. In fact I encourage you not to overdo it. Sometimes less is more. Folks don't want to sleep in a shell shop or in the bowels of a fishing boat.

Secondly, theme is important to the type of customer you want to attract. If you search B&B brokers on the Internet, you will see that there are some sites that only cater to high-end Inns. These are inns that are considerably more expensive than a standard inn of the same area and are obviously looking for a moneyed clientele. This is fine and dandy, but for most couple-run operations, the property cost, décor, and amenities offered by these showcase inns can be hard to afford.

Michelle's Thought: A bit about naming your inn. This may be a no-brainer if you're moving into a historic home or area: "The Hathaway House" for a pastoral family home, or "Central Park Bed & Breakfast" can be obvious and practical name choices. Check nearby for similarly named inns, as this could confuse your guests, and could also lead to mail, website and GPS-system location overlap and uncertainty.

Another observation is the number of inns with European décor and services. With the dollar losing value to many international currencies, foreign travelers visiting the U.S. are on an upswing. Catering to this clientele can be rewarding, but carries added cost and challenges in advertising, language, and cuisine. The point is the theme of your inn should be a successful marriage of what is comfortable and homey to you, and what represents the character of the geography and flavor of the local area.

How many rooms do you want?

This is an important question that can probably be resolved by answering a few others first. Like, are you going to run things alone or do you have a partner? Do you want to hire (and be ready to fire) others? What will the market in your area support?

Even if you are a workaholic, operating a B&B by yourself is not recommended. The varied tasks and time requirements necessary to operate a B&B successfully can be a challenge even for the most organized and supportive couple. If you feel you must, you should probably keep it to four rooms or less. I have seen B&B's with only two rooms that are quite successful single-person operations. I have also stayed at a four room B&B where the couple that ran it also worked regular jobs Monday thru Friday. The point is to realistically match the workload created by the number of rooms you have, to the time and capability of the people operating it.

Our Inn has six rooms, and when we are busy, it takes both of us a full day to complete the chores necessary to run the business; do the shopping, bookkeeping, laundry, housekeeping, cooking, gardening, facility and equipment maintenance, as well as guest relations are just a few of the required daily tasks. This is all we do. If either one of us had an outside job, I believe the other would feel overwhelmed and our satisfaction with being innkeepers would fall greatly.

If you want an Inn with more than five or six rooms you will probably need to hire help, a chef, a maid, perhaps a desk clerk, even a gardener. Are you prepared to manage personnel? Can you hire and fire? What about taxes and workers comp? What if someone calls in sick or quits unexpectedly? The point is, you move from being a full-time innkeeper yourself to being a manager and boss. Does this fit in with your Goals and Desires list?

Keep in mind that most inns that you find for sale, or houses you may convert into a B&B, are going to provide you with four to six guest rooms. This is the perfect size inn for a couple to manage while still allowing time for personal pursuits.

Inn shopping note: When looking at potential Inns remember that you have to live there too. Is there space for you personally? How much privacy will you have from your guests? I recommend that you have living quarters separate from the main inn. This can be under the same roof, but it should be private.
You will need a place to get away and be comfortable. If you want to walk around in your underwear you should be able to do so without encountering a surprised guest.

Do you want a staff?

We have discussed the need for a staff to some degree already. The size of your inn, and whether or not you will have a restaurant or gift shop will guide your decision. The main issue with staff is in personnel management. Advertising for employees, interviewing, pay and benefits, and staff scheduling will all be necessary. Having a staff may require that you deduct income taxes and/or pay social security and workers comp for your employees. In most cases, the assistance of an accountant can be helpful if you are unfamiliar with these requirements.

When hiring staff, it is also important that you attract employees that exemplify your business personality. You guests will inevitably encounter staff and they should be warm and friendly, displaying the demeanor that you desire. It does no good for you to be an excellent host while your staff could care less. Just as your décor and amenities add to the enjoyment of your guests, the friendliness of your staff is part of your presentation as well. Guests will remember if they are treated well and their needs are met, and consider this when choosing to return or recommend your inn to others.

Unless you have experience in personnel management and payroll requirements, you should get help here. Having employees can be a fun and rewarding experience, but it also can be a headache. If you are just starting out, I suggest that you personally handle as many of the tasks necessary to run your business as possible. This allows you to learn what is involved in operating a B&B and ensures things get done the way you want.

Michelle's Thought: Hiring others to do the "dirty work" is definitely an advantage, if you can afford it, however, there are many advantages to doing it yourself when you first start out, not the least of them financial. One thing I hated about my traditional jobs is the seemingly nonchalant way I was asked to do very difficult things in an impossible time period. Many of my supervisors obviously had NO idea what I was faced with, because they had NEVER DONE IT. Most had never even seen ME do it. There is great value in knowing how much effort and time go into ANY given task before asking anyone else to do it. This way you'll know personally what your employees need, in materials and in support, to do what they do, and they will respect and trust you more for it, too.

Do you want a restaurant?

This is a big one. Most innkeepers I have talked to that have restaurants as part of their business say that the restaurant quickly becomes the biggest workload. Restaurants can be very profitable and can draw guests to stay at your inn, as well as bring in the locals. The truth is, however, that a restaurant is a business unto itself and adds concerns such as licensing, state inspection, liability issues if alcohol is served, the need for reliable suppliers, waste management problems, and purchasing food in large quantities.

If you are purchasing an inn that has an operating restaurant, I suggest you ask for printed policies and procedures that may already have been established. Consider how long employees, kitchen and wait staff have been employed, and if they intend to stay on. Look at the financials for the restaurant operation and weigh if the added work volume is worth your time and energy. You will put in many hours to maintain a successful restaurant, and as I said, you should expect it to become the primary part of your operation.

If you don't have food service and management experience, I encourage you to carefully consider if operating a restaurant, and the added work it entails, matches your Goals and Desires list.

One thing you could consider if you have the facilities to do so is offering private parties or hosting meetings. This is a good source of additional income, and you can plan relatively well in advance what you need to accommodate hosting them. You will know how many folks are attending, if a meal is desired, the menu requested, and the time frame guests will be in your house. This allows you to control costs and more importantly, your time.

A final thought on restaurants. They are highly regulated businesses. You should expect to have to meet health department, alcohol control board, fire department, and local government requirements. For example, a standard cook top that may have been okay for a B&B operation will probably need to be upgraded for restaurant use with commercial equipment including a hood (fire extinguishing) system, grease collection systems, and quarterly health inspection requirements.

Do you want to host weddings and special events?

As I have said, hosting small parties, dinners, or weddings can be a great way to add to your business. Beyond having the room necessary to do so, you should also consider potential conflicts. Do you have separate bathroom facilities that attendees can use? How much interference will the event generate to overnight guests? Do you have the parking necessary? Do you have the exterior grounds for an outside wedding? What about tent rental? These are only some of the questions to consider.

Michelle and I do offer private party services, but we are careful in treating our overnight customers as our priority. We have one room on the ground floor that we use for a changing/coat room and bathroom facilities for attendees when we host a party. This means we cannot rent that particular room overnight on party days, unless the folks who are having the event want a room for the night. Also, and noise generated from the event can have an impact on our other guests. The ability for overnight guests to quietly enjoy the common areas of the inn is compromised when a party is taking place. This can generate a bad experience for them if peace and quiet, or a romantic evening by the fire was part of what they were looking for.

If you are going to offer special services, you should consider the time and resources involved in doing so and come up with a formula that allows you to determine what to charge. You may find that by the time it is all over and done, it was not worth your effort. In most cases, however, hosting parties is a nice way of adding to your income and potentially enhancing your overnight bookings in the future.

Note: When calculating the charge for party services you should have a base rate and time limit with the ability to add charges as requirements necessitate. Our base rate is $200.00 with a three-hour time limit including set-up. One thing we did not initially consider (that we now do), is the use of our glasses and dishes and/or kitchen facilities. We have found that party guests will enjoy using these items fully, and when the party is finished; depart, leaving the clean up to us. You may, as we have, compensate for this by adding a pantry and/or kitchen fee to cover this added workload.

Do you want a gift shop?

Having a gift shop, or area, can be a nice way to offer your guests locally produced products and even crafts that you make yourself. The added income from sale of these items will probably be minimal, but guests seem to enjoy having them available. Who does not like to shop? Michelle and I offer locally made syrup, souvenir items, wines, post cards, and even our personalized coffee mugs at our "gift corner". We do not try to make any great profit on these items, it is simply something that our guests find quaint, and Michelle enjoys finding new and interesting items to offer.

Should you have the room, you may consider a full-fledged gift shop. This again is a distraction from the primary B&B operation, and can become a small business unto itself. If you are crafty, and make quilts or wood furniture for example, a gift shop can be a way for you to offer your products to the public. You may even add the ability to purchase your items on your web site if you like. Just remember, you will need to keep good records on the income produced from the sale of such items separately from the revenue generated from renting rooms.

How much property do you want to own?

The land associated with your inn is an important factor for your business. If you have only a small lot with neighbors close by, you may not have the room for weddings or outside parties. If you are in a rural setting and have a small pond or secluded area where you can put a hot tub, guests will greatly enjoy these types of amenities. Do you have lake access? What about bike or hiking trails? How about a tennis court?

The possibilities are endless, and usually dictated by the character of the property you acquire. An inn that serves a college for example, may be on a busy road and have limited exterior grounds for your guests to enjoy but will not be detrimental to business. A country inn may have extensive acreage where guests can wander off into nature and enjoy the local flora and fauna, and give you the ability to offer more services. You should simply consider what the vision of your inn looks like and search for a property that allows you to make your dreams a reality. Just remember, more land equals a higher initial purchase price, increased grounds maintenance, and higher property taxes.

What kind of guests do you want to attract?

This may seem like a trick question. Paying ones, of course. But what I am talking about is the character of the guests you envision visiting your inn. If you are seeking to cater to the rich, you will need to present a facility with amenities that the rich enjoy. This may mean having a 24-hour desk clerk, offering gourmet meals, or offering spa services. If you are seeking the sporting traveler, you may need to accommodate the type of equipment your guests use. Do you have a place to safely house bicycles, skis, snowmobiles, motor cycles, fishing gear? Do you have an inventory of items for them to use? Can these items be rented nearby if a guest requires?

Believe it or not, your vision of the type of guests you desire to stay with you will have an impact on how you advertise, decorate, and the services you provide. If a southern inn that offers access to great fishing is your vision, you will attract people who enjoy fishing. If you see yourself running a secluded inn in the country, you will attract couples and those looking for romance or those seeking quiet rest. If you see yourself near popular attractions that cater to kids, you will attract vacationing families.

Considering the type of guest you are hoping to attract will further guide you in answering all of the questions posed in this chapter and ultimately, result in your satisfaction, or dissatisfaction, with being an innkeeper. Remember, one of the greatest rewards of being an innkeeper is the people you meet. You definitely want to attract guests that you can relate to and have an understanding of what it takes for them to enjoy their stay, but you will ultimately get all types of visitors. If you disconnect from your guests because you dislike their interests, it will have a negative impact on their experience and yours. You should try to relate to all of your guests equally, enjoying the new knowledge and experiences they bring. The effort will enrich you beyond the value of their room bill.

CHAPTER 5

Selecting Your Inn

Location, Location, Location.

Choosing the right location for your inn in one of your most important decisions. You should research this carefully considering many things. First and foremost is; what is your market? Are you catering to skiers? How far are the slopes? Fishermen, what access do you have to the water? Families, How far are you from attractions?

If you are buying an established inn, the current owners should be able to tell you what draws their primary customers. For Michelle and me it is the private academy next door. We get over 80% of our business from visitors who are somehow affiliated with the school; parents of students, potential students, alumni, attendees of special events, summer seminars and conferences, and temporary staff.

> *Michelle's Thought: We were lucky enough to move into a town I knew very well—the one I had grown up in. If you're starting out in a place not so familiar to you, I urge you to get out there in it. The smaller the community, the faster the good news will spread: "There's a new bed & breakfast in town and I met the owner, he/she's really nice." Get to know the locals, and patronize their businesses. Check out the local library, post office, school(s), even churches and establish good relationships along the way. Ask humbly, speak softly, and introduce yourself to your neighbors if they don't beat you to it. It's amazing how far small, kind gestures will go towards starting your business off on the right foot.*

Knowing your market will assist you greatly in developing projections of income and growth. One thing you should definitely do is to determine the average occupancy of other inns in the area. Some innkeepers will be happy to share this information with you. Another good source would be the local chamber of commerce or lodging association. They usually have a good idea of how tourism is going in the local area.

We will talk about developing a business plan later, but knowing your expected annual occupancy percentage will drive many of your calculations and projections. So this research is a must.

Another consideration is property access. Can visitors get to you easily in all types of weather conditions? What about signage? If you are off the highway, how are folks going to find you? Locally, we have an inn that occasionally has its business interrupted due to work on a nearby dam. Guests can still access the inn by a round about loop, but the innkeeper must install additional signage to properly direct traffic to them.

Another location issue is privacy. Michelle and I looked at an inn that was fantastic. It was a historic house that had many charms. The problem was that it was in the middle of a residential neighborhood with a two-story house on one side, and a low-rise condominium on the other. Both structures posed view issues from the guest rooms and caused privacy issues as rooms on the second and third floors were now at an eye-level view to the neighbors. Sunbathing in private in the backyard, or discreetly using the hot tub, would be impossible.

One important consideration on location is for you as the innkeeper. How far away is the grocery store? Bank? Gas station? Garage? Home improvement store? Hairdresser? You will have to do all the regular things you do now even as an innkeeper, so keep your quality of life in mind as well. Also, consider that your distance from fire and EMS services, as well as a reliable fire department water supply, may have an impact on your renovations and local fire safety requirements, as well as your business insurance.

Buying verses Renting

This is a big one. The nice thing about running a bed & breakfast is that you work where you live. This has many advantages, such a no more commuting, you are the boss, you can dress as you like, and most of the expenses to operate the B&B also benefit you personally. You get a roof over your head, at least half of your grocery bill is for the business (but you get to eat too), and the cable TV, internet access, water, telephone, heat and light you offer your guests all benefit you too. The down side is that you have no pension plan, health insurance or other big-company benefits.

If you are already retired and collecting a pension, or if you have significant savings to carry you through your golden years, this will be less of an issue. Most of us are not in such flush circumstances, however, and we need to do a little planning. For a B&B owner, most of your future worth will come from the increased value of the inn property, and to some extent, the business you build. You should not, however, expect to get much more than your initial and ongoing operating investment back from simply selling the business without the property. I have spoken to many innkeeper/property owners, who planned from the beginning to reap the benefit of increased property values at some later date. If you rent, you will not have this valuable benefit when you decide to retire (again).

Buying verses renting your B&B has many of the same positives and negatives as doing so for your home. It is your home after all. If you rent, your start-up costs will be less, as you will most likely only need to provide first and last month's rent and a security deposit, and depending on the structure of your lease, your renovation costs, property and structural maintenance costs, some of your utilities, and even insurance may be covered by the property owner. Keep in mind, however, that you will also have to answer to the property owner for your use of the property, and you may be restricted on some business operations such as operating a restaurant on the premises, or even if you can allow pets.

If you decide to rent, you should carefully word your lease to allow you as the business owner as much freedom in your operations as possible. Make sure all parties involved have specified, in writing, what is included and allowed, and more importantly, what is not. Landlords have a way of interfering with business, as it is the long-term value of the property that is important to them. They will not want you to do anything that will limit the potential market to sell the property, and do not want to spend buckets of cash replacing appliances or painting and improving the property. One thing is certain, if you do not specify these types of responsibilities in advance, you as the business owner will be on the hook when the refrigerator craps out or the septic tank overflows.

Buying your inn is by far your best option, if you can swing it. Once you own it, you can do what you like, when you like. You get to choose the house color, the best appliances, if you are going to allow pets, have a hot tub, what your sign looks like, and all the other decisions that a landlord may put restrictions on. You also get the financial benefits inherent with property ownership, including any increased value of the property over time.

Note: Even if you own the property, you should expect restrictions on use as mandated by laws and ordinances, and the rules of any licensing bodies such as the health department.

CHAPTER 6

Renovation, Inspections, Licensing

No matter if you buy or rent, unless the property is already running as an established inn, you will have some level of renovation work ahead of you. Please, please, please, do your homework on this topic before you sign a lease or purchase agreement.

As a Fire Marshal for a large southern municipality, one of my duties was to ensure Life Safety Code compliance of businesses. In most cases, existing businesses can continue to operate without major new building code requirements being mandated. This makes sense if you consider something like newer building codes that have been adopted on the engineering of house foundations. If these new requirements were placed on all structures in town, very old houses with stone foundations would have to be torn down and rebuilt to comply. You should be careful though, as most building codes mandate that if over a certain percentage of renovation takes place, say greater then 30% of the existing structure, compliance with the newer standards will be necessary. Matters pertaining to the Life Safety Code, however, do not enjoy this "grand fathering" protection.

I had a young couple that had just purchased a historic home in the downtown area with the intent of converting it to a lovely B&B. They had already closed on the property and were now in the process of planning their renovations. Their improvements had little to do with the exterior of the house and more to do with interior changes. This, they believed, would make the whole process much easier, and from a building code standpoint, it did. The problem arose when they indicated their business plan was structured on making what was now a six-bedroom home into a ten-room inn. Now I won't belabor the details too much here, but this opened a can of worms that nearly shattered them.

To operate a lodging facility with ten or more rooms added a great number of requirements, most of them very costly, such as adding a fire alarm and fire sprinkler system. Further, the requirements for adding fire escapes to each room now impacted the exterior of the structure, and put the property owners dangerously close to that 30% renovation mark that would open the door to numerous other mandated building changes. In the end, they were forced to open a business that was far less than what they had planned (five rooms only), and was no longer projected to generate anywhere near the income they had hoped.

My suggestions for you to avoid such surprises is to hire a few professionals before you enter into any agreements, or spend any major dollars on a B&B. Hire a real-estate attorney and a design professional and/or a well-respected contractor to walk you through the processes. The money you spend on their services now can save you a bundle in the future. Even before you hire any professionals, you can ask for a meeting with your local building and fire officials to discuss your plans and any concerns they may have. The education you gain will be highly valuable. You should also see if there is a local planning board and research any requirement they may have in approving your business plan.

After doing your research you can hire a contractor and start actually making changes to your Inn. My advice here is simple. Don't take on any job yourself that you are not 100% confident you can complete properly and safely. Many a haphazard wiring job has resulted in an unintended fire. Hire only reputable contractors who are licensed, insured, and will provide in writing a detailed list of the work to be done and the guaranteed cost. And make sure, this is your responsibility, that they get all the proper permits and job inspections that are required.

You will find that most B&B guests prefer a private bathroom, a feature you will not find in most existing homes. If you do nothing else, renovating all of your rooms to include a private bath (minimum shower, sink, and toilet), is a good investment.

One last piece of advice on renovations; don't spend more on renovation than you expect you can recoup in the first three to five years of being in business. When you are profitable, you can consider additional renovations. You may also find that you will discover additional things that you want to include on the second round of improvements. Perhaps a neighboring inn has whirlpool tubs and you want to offer them too, or you have a sun porch that you want to enclose to make a tearoom?

Construction costs today are high, and getting higher all the time. Permitting, inspection, and the mandates of the building and life safety codes grow every year. If you can find a property that is close to ideal for your plans without having to perform severe renovations, you will have far fewer headaches and keep a lot more cash in your pocket.

Don't forget ADA (Americans with Disabilities Act) requirements when planning renovations. Most states will require you provide some level of accommodation for the disabled, including ease of building access as well as specified parking.

Regulatory Requirements and Licenses

No matter where you want to run your bed and breakfast, you will have some form of regulatory agency to contend with, and you should expect that some type of business licensing would be required. If you are lucky these "red tape" issues will be minimal. You should at minimum expect to be inspected by the fire department and health department, and need to obtain a small business license. If you also have a restaurant, a food service permit and liquor license will also be necessary.

Permits and licenses are a necessary evil. While they may pose an aggravation to you, they indicate to your customers that your operations are safe and have met minimum standards for operation. They also protect you should you need to make a claim on your insurance of if a guest were to sue you for a mishap like food poisoning.

Michelle and I had to make presentations for approval of our B&B to the town Planning Board and fire department. We were required to obtain a State food service license and register as a small business, and apply to collect state meals and rooms tax. The town building official, state health department, and state Americans with disabilities compliance director all performed inspections prior to our opening for business.

I strongly suggest that you determine in advance the licensing and regulatory requirements you will need to meet in your area to open your business. Do no cheat on this step, as regulatory agencies usually have the power to close you down and can impose a fine for non-compliance. When writing a purchase offer or negotiating a lease, you should include a provision that lets you off the hook if you are unable to successfully obtain all required permits and inspections. Sometimes even established business owners are innocently in non-compliance with newly adopted regulations and surprises can arise.

Licensing, permits, and inspections is definitely another area where spending time in advance meeting with the officials involved in enforcing the requirements will provide you with some very valuable knowledge. Be gracious, tell the truth about what you are planning, and be prepared to pay any fees necessary to operate a legitimate business.

CHAPTER 7

Beds, Linens, and Towels

Beds

When Michelle and I began the process of purchasing furniture for our inn, we put the highest priority on beds and linens; after all we were opening a Bed and Breakfast! BED is right in the name, so we wanted ours to be special. I am not talking about frames and headboards here, you can use antiques if you desire (they may require some modification). I am referring to the mattresses, sheets, blankets and quilts, pillows, covers and bedspreads.

The foundation of a fantastic bed is the mattress set. I recommend purchasing the best mattresses you can afford, and that should be the best available. Your beds are the workhorses of the service you are selling to the public, and as such will take the most abuse. People will sleep, sit, jump, eat, have relations, and just about anything else you can think of on your beds. They need to hold up and be just as comfortable to your 100th guest as they were to your first.

Early on, Michelle and I had a guest who was an ex-football linebacker. In the morning after he checked out, we went to turn his room and found the mattress he had slept on was markedly dented. Thankfully, we had purchased top-of-the line commercial mattresses, and it recovered after we turned it for a few days. Had it not rebounded, it would certainly needed to be replaced and we would have been faced with trying to charge our guest for the damage, an embarrassing and uncertain proposition for sure.

The mattress sets we bought were high-quality, commercial Posturepedics, also used by five-star hotels. They are designed for hotel use and have a quarterly turning and rotation schedule printed on tags sewn to each corner, something you should follow to get maximum service from your investment. This type of mattress is not cheap as far as price goes, but we have never regretted having them. It is so very gratifying having a guest tell us at breakfast that their bed was the most comfortable they have ever slept on, and this happens to us quite often.

When we purchased our beds, we started by looking at the usual retail outlets and department stores. We found very nice premium mattress sets, but they all had two problems. One, they were not designed for commercial use, and two, they were quite expensive. Soon we began researching hotel and motel suppliers to see what was available through them. We looked mainly at five-star hotel suppliers, not discount chain-type suppliers. What we found was we could purchase the best quality commercial mattress sets at about half the cost of the finest personal-use department store brands.

There are many fantastic hotel suppliers you can research online. You can get most of the commercial items you will need easily and have them shipped right to your inn door. You should pay careful attention, however, to the suppliers' minimum purchase requirements. In the case of the beds we selected, a minimum order of ten (for each size) was required to get the pricing listed, and as we only needed six, this presented a problem. We got lucky, though, when I called the supplier and asked if we could purchase less than the minimum number. This is where it pays to be personable and nice to people. Although the policy on minimum numbers was not negotiable, the fantastic customer service representative noted that a major New York hotel had just placed an order for a large number of the same mattress set we wanted, and in a few minutes, she got approval to add our six beds to the same order. This made us feel very grateful, and we got the top-of-the-line, name brand beds we wanted at a fantastic price.

A note on bed sizes: Keep in mind that you will have to stock linens for each bed size you offer. I recommend queen as your primary size, as it is what most guests are used to sleeping on at home, and the space needed for the frame and headboard works well, even in smaller floor area rooms. Having pillows of all the same size is also helpful in this regard. You should also stock a few hypoallergenic and pillows of differing thickness, as they may be requested.

Linens

Now that you have ordered your beds you will need linens. Your two top considerations here are quality and quantity. Quality is again something you should spare no expense on. That being said, in my opinion you can also go too far. You should definitely purchase high thread-count, cotton or cotton/polyester mix sheets. The mix sheets will wrinkle less, but also feel a bit stiffer when slept on. 100% cotton sheets are extremely comfortable, but will require extra effort to get them folded directly from a hot dryer and/or ironing. As a rule, however, the better the sheets, the longer their service life.

The color, or colors, of your sheets should also be considered here. Your guests will inevitably stain your sheets and pillowcases and bleaching will become necessary. If you have color sheets, bleach will fade them over time. For this reason, Michelle and I decided to use only white sheets and pillowcases. It simplifies laundering, and they do not fade. You can add color to your beds with your blankets, spreads, and shams. Keep in mind that using bleach will shorten the service life of your linens and will not remove all stains.

Note: A good stain pre-treatment, and a commercial make-up remover should also be on your laundry room shelf.

Speaking of laundry, are you going to do it yourself? For larger operations of ten or more rooms, a linen service may be an option, but look out for linen quality and thread count. High quality linens may be available from these type services, but at a premium cost. For most couple run inns you will most likely do your own laundry and should consider your washer and dryer carefully. Standard residential washers and dryers are fine for your personal laundry, but may not be appropriate for inn keeping. Residential-style washers usually use a lot of water and the agitator inside will shorten the life of your linens, and most dryers are of a standard residential load size and can use a lot of energy per load.

The solution may be to purchase a set of the newer technology washer and dryer sets available through the major home improvement chains. We recommend front loading machines, as they have a larger than standard capacity. Look for equipment with good energy ratings, low water use, and cost-saving technology such as 'Silver Care'. The washer we use requires little or no bleach and gets our whites fantastically clean. It also spins the load at such a high speed that the load feels almost dry when you move it from the washer to the dryer. The dryer has technology that monitors the drying time and shuts the unit off if the load is dry before the timer has elapsed. All of these features save us time, and more importantly, money.

Now let's talk briefly about the quantity of linens you will need. Unless you want to do laundry everyday, I recommend three full sets (fitted, flat, and two pillowcases) for each bed in your inn. This allows for a set to be on the bed, a fresh set on the linen closet shelf, and a set in the wash. Having this quantity of linens will also provide for ample rotation that will prolong service life.

Mattress and Pillow Covers

After careful laundering, covers will greatly add to the service life of your mattresses and pillows. Please do not go cheap here and be tempted to purchase the inexpensive plastic covers; your guests will feel (and hear) them through the linens, and they do not breathe at all, making your beds and pillows uncomfortable to sleep on. There are higher quality cloth covers available that are waterproof and will protect your mattresses and pillows from flow-through staining. They will also make your beds more sanitary.

Towels

The same things I mentioned for sheets and pillowcases apply to your towels. You may be tempted to get various colors, but this will complicate laundering and stain removal. Also, quality is of utmost importance. Guests will notice if the towel they dry off with is cheap and thin, they will also notice if they are thick and luxurious. They will not care if they are blue, green, or white.

> *Michelle's Thought: There are a couple of schools of thought on towel quality; some innkeepers believe that thick and delicious towels will get stolen, and that smaller, lightweight towels can be used instead. While we admittedly don't have the most luxurious towels you can buy, we erred on the side of better quality, and have never regretted it, nor have ever had one stolen.*

The quantity formula used for sheets and pillowcases also works here, a set on the towel rack; a set in the linen closet, and a set in the wash should be the minimum. Having a dozen or so extra bath towels is also a good idea, as some guests do request extras.

A note on where to buy sheets and pillowcases, and towels: Most hotel/motel suppliers offer linens, pillows, and towels. However, unless you know exactly what you are getting, we do not recommend purchasing them in this manner. Most of the big box stores sell high-quality towels and linens, and if you are lucky, you will even find them on sale. Purchasing these items in person allows you to see and feel the quality, and with towels, hold them up and see the size and style. Purchasing close by also allows you to readily replace damaged linens without having to meet supplier minimum-order quantities.

Michelle and I purchased our sheets from the same major New York hotel supplier as our beds, and we are very satisfied with the quality and longevity.

We originally purchased our towels from a different motel supplier based upon their description of them being their "best five-star quality towels." We were, however, extremely disappointed when they arrived, as they were small, thin, and, we felt, substandard. Our disappointment was further aggravated when we had to pay the cost of shipping to return them. We immediately went to a local department store and got fantastic premium quality towel sets that look and feel great, and cost us about half of what we originally spent, and our guests compliment us on them daily.

CHAPTER 8

Décor and Amenities

Decorating

Decorating is the fun part! This is where you let your personality mix with the style of house you chose for your inn. Most of you will already have an idea of what type of feel you want in your inn. For some of you it will be a country feel, for others it may be European or even modern style. My recommendation, here again, is to visit numerous inns and see what style appeals to you. It is important that the décor of your inn reflect your personality as much as possible; you will be living there after all, and it should not only be comfortable for your guests but also for you and your family.

Michelle and I joined two innkeeper associations in our area that allow for mutual support and shared advertising costs to drive tourism to our area. One of the benefits of belonging to such organizations is that our meetings are hosted at a different member inn each month. This gives other innkeepers an opportunity to see what other inns are offering to their guests as far as amenities go and a feel for the experience their guests receive. It is a great way to get ideas that you may want to, or not want to, incorporate into your inn.

At one inn we visited that had a distinctive European style we noticed that there were floor towels placed next to both sides of the beds. The innkeeper explained that his clientele was largely European and that since the floors in many European hotels are sometimes cold so they would place floor towels next to the bed so the guests would not have to put their feet directly on the cold floor when they got up to put on their slippers. The floors in his inn were carpeted so I was a little confused but it seems the extra effort was appreciated by his guests and added to their feeing of comfort so he always did it.

Another observation was at an inn we visited where the couple that ran it had spent a number of years prior to becoming innkeepers traveling the world. In their travels they picked up many souvenirs of their adventures with the intent of using them as accents to their inns décor. The knickknacks were very interesting and each had a story of the exotic location the couple had visited and opened the door to many fun conversations. The problem was there was just too many of them. Everywhere you looked or sat there were fragile items on the tables or shelves. I was scared I would bump one with my elbow and ruin an icon of a great travel memory. If I felt that way, I can imagine their guests did too.

Our recommendation when decorating is to start with the philosophy that less is more. A simply appointed room can be more comfortable for a guest than an over-decorated one. Of course you will have a bed or beds with headboards, spreads and shams, one or two end tables, perhaps a chair and writing table, a dresser, and a few pictures on the walls. Beyond this, go slow with the extras. In our inn each room is named after a different New England state, so we have included items from each state as part of the décor. A few books on state flora and fauna, commemorative display plates, dried flowers, etc, but very sparingly. The pictures (mostly paintings) also stay with the general New England theme. The floors are hard wood accented with a few area rugs and the bed covers are where we also add color and texture.

By keeping our guest rooms more simply appointed, they present as clean and tidy and allow our guests to spread out and more fully enjoy the space. They are also easier to clean after the guests depart, something you will come to appreciate as time goes by.

Note: We just want to touch on the true-life fact that stealing does occur. It may be just an ashtray or bath towel, but it may also be pictures or knick-knacks. The best approach for you is to not decorate with anything that you wouldn't mind being broken, or anything irreplaceable, like a family heirloom.

Finally, don't forget the outside of your inn. You should have good curb appeal to arriving guests. Window boxes with seasonal flowers or attractive nighttime lighting can be very inviting to your guests. Keep your lawn and foliage well groomed. Repair loose shingles and touch-up painted surfaces as soon as they need it. Keep your parking areas clean, wash windows, and keep after fingerprints on entrance doors. All of these things will make a good first impression to your guests.

Guest Goodies

Although they are not décor items, guest goodies do add to the presentation of your rooms and the overall experience of your guests. A few well-placed chocolates on the bedside table tell your guests that you appreciate them. Having a few bottles of water on the dresser for your guests to take vitamins before bed or to refresh themselves at night without having to wander to the kitchen will also be appreciated. In the bathroom, offering small soaps of even travel shampoos and conditioner is a nice addition, although most guests do bring their own personal care items. Just having a few of these items along with a fresh tooth brush and paste if a guest forgets them may be enough.

For economy, Michelle placed dispensers in each of our showers with shampoo, conditioner, and body soap. Judging by the refill rate, about half of our guests partake of them. Later, we started placing small-boxed soaps in the bathrooms, and find that most guests use them either for bathing or hand washing. The cost is minimal if you purchase your soaps in bulk, so I do recommend having hard soaps available. Offering travel-sized shampoo and conditioner can be expensive and is a mater of choice.

Here is a Chris pet peeve. Do not cheap out on the quality of toilet paper! Yes, buying quilted, extra-soft toilet paper is more expensive than the stuff offered by most hotel supply warehouses, but it is worth it. The extra comfort your guests' experience when using the soft stuff can solidify their good impression of your inn and bring them back in the future. Just the same, being cheap in the bathroom can reflect poorly on your guests experience and cause them to try another inn next time. Your guests are paying more to stay at a B&B than an interstate motel, and as such, expect a bit more luxury.

Michelle and I did have one guest that said we offered too many extras and suggested we cut our costs by eliminating them. She based her advice on personal experience in operating a small business where her business partner gave away a lot of promotional items and in turn bankrupted the business. This advice, although a little over-cautious, does have value when you are just starting out. Provide some extras that add value and comfort to your guests stay but don't get carried away giving away coffee mugs that cost $5 a pop.

Services

Services are extras you may offer your guests that usually incur an extra charge. If, for example, you offer spa services like massages, facials, or manicures, there will be a cost associated with staff and supplies. Knowing both what you intend to offer and having a pricelist available is important. Some inns do offer sporting goods like canoes, snowshoes, or even bicycles to their guests at no additional charge. This is fantastic, as it draws guests to you and limits their hassle in renting such equipment. Keep in mind, however, that items like life vests and maintenance of such equipment will be necessary. Also, folks like your spa employees may require licensing and you may have other state regulations that have to be met. Do your research if you plan to be and inn and spa. Perhaps partnering with a locally established salon or spa would be a better way to go, and you can offer relax-and-stay packages that will keep guests coming back to your inn.

Another area partnership that can be worthwhile is for outdoor activities. Why buy kayaks or bicycles for your guests to use when an outfitter may be just down the street? Outfitters usually offer guides for those who are unfamiliar with the area, and they, of course, incur the cost of purchasing and maintaining the equipment. You will find that these types of businesses are very interested in working with you, and everyone benefits.

The bottom line is that offering extra services to your guests can be both a blessing and a curse if you are selling your inn based upon them. If an outfitter upsets a guest, they may blame you and not recommend you to others. If they have a good experience on their adventure, the opposite may occur. You should always try to provide the best for your guests whether you are lending them a bike or sending them to an outfitter. Ask them to provide feedback on their experience, and always look for ways to improve their visit.

Technology

Do you put a television in every room or not? This is a personal choice and should be discussed at the time you decorate. Our experience has been that most folks find comfort in having a TV available for viewing, even if they never turn it on. Outdoor types may want to check the weather. Relax and stay guests may not care to know what is happening in the world for a few days. To that end, we did place TV's with DVD players in each of our guest rooms, but we tried, where possible, to not make them a focal point.

In some rooms, our televisions are in armoires that can be closed to make them less visible to our guests, in others we mounted them on wall stands for convenience. The bottom line is that the guests can choose to view a television or not, but the TV itself is an extra, not the highlight of the room. By choice, we do not have a TV in any of the guests' common areas of the inn. If someone wants to view a show, they can do so in the privacy of their own room. This allows other guests to enjoy the quiet of a fire, or simply relax and read a book in one of our window seats without a TV distracting them in the background.

No conversation on technology would be complete without talking about wireless Internet. The bottom line here is you should definitely offer it. I don't know if not offering televisions would have an impact on whether a guest stays with us or not, but I know for sure not having wireless Internet access would. This is an inexpensive service for your guests, and almost everyone who stays with us asks if we offer it. Routers are inexpensive, and you will almost certainly already be paying for cable access as part of your business. You should provide Internet access free of charge and advertise such on all of your printed materials and your web site.

CHAPTER 9

Writing Your Business Plan

Okay, we have put this off long enough. All successful businesses have a written business plan, and you will want one too. We probably should have covered this part earlier, but now that you have thought about so many particulars for your B&B, you will be much more enthusiastic writing your business plan, and enthusiasm is important.

Business plans are road maps to your success, and are a vital part of obtaining needed financing or allaying any concerns that may arise through the permitting and municipal approval processes. There are many good guides to writing a business plan, and you can even find templates and examples on the web. I strongly suggest you invest some time in reading a few example plans and check out a book that guides you through the process from the library. Here is a brief overview of what a business plan is all about.

Most business plans begin with a short profile of the business you intend to start, including a description of your product or service, where your customers will come from, current trends in the industry, and your pricing. If you have done the research I have suggested in this book, you should already be able to answer most of these points. You should do so in your own words, and as concisely as possible without compromising a positive tone.

You should have already given consideration to your choice of business structure. You may choose a sole proprietorship where even though you have a business name, you and the business are one and the same legally. You may choose to operate as a partnership where you and at least one other person share the business risks and responsibilities. Another option is to form a corporation where shareholders own the business, even if it's just you. Finally, and what seems to be most popular among small innkeepers, is to form a Limited Liability Company or LLC. LLC's provide the business owners with personal liability protection like corporations, without the legal and financial restrictions associated with shareholders. You will need to understand the differences between business structures and pick one that will properly format your business plan.

For the prospective innkeeper, one of the most important elements of your business plan is your pricing, or rate structure. This will become the cornerstone of your business plan. Knowing that your room rates are competitive to your market, based on your expected occupancy, and able to provide the income necessary to be successful, will guide every decision you make, and for that matter, the decisions of any lenders or creditors. The formula looks like this:

Average Room Rate × Number of Rooms × Number of Operating Days × Expected Occupancy – Projected Operating Costs = Profit or Loss

This is an important calculation, so let's look at an example. Say that you have determined that you can charge $150.00 a night on average for your rooms, and you have a six-room inn. Doing good research and talking to other innkeepers in the area, you have determined that the average yearly occupancy for your chosen location is 25%, and through further honest research you anticipate that the monthly operating costs for your inn, including mortgage, utilities, groceries, maintenance, (everything!), will be approx $7000.00. Let's use the formula to see if you have a viable business.

$150 × 6 rooms = $900 × 351 days (allowing for a two-week vacation) = $315,900 × 25% expected occupancy = $78,975 gross annual income – $7000 monthly operating costs × 12 months, or $84,000 annually = a net loss of $5,025 annually.

So now what do we do? Well, you can adjust your room rates to cover the deficiency, but that may price you out of the market. You can make up the difference with a gift shop or by offering other add-on's, you can review your operating budget to trim your expenses, or you can simply move on and find a better market and location for your business. Regardless, your goal should be to have your anticipated revenue exceed your operating costs by a comfortable percentage. There are always expenses you did not plan for, and acts of God such as weather emergencies or even local events such as a burst water main that can have a negative impact on your projected occupancy.

Note: Remember, you will have high occupancy months and low occupancy months. The goal is to project your yearly average and budget so the profits earned in the busy months can carry you through the slow ones where you book a loss.

Most sources will advise you to not plan on making a profit your first year in business. If the average occupancy for inns in your area is 25%, you will be doing well to reach perhaps 15% your first year in business. It takes time for folks to get to know you are there and for you to learn how, when, and where to advertise. If you reach the average occupancy the second year, you are doing great! My suggestion would be to plan on at least three years before you match the average occupancy of your competitors. This means you will need some cash in reserve to cover those start-up losses without going out of business. These reserve funds should be accurately reflected in the financial profile section of your business plan.

Let's press on with building your business plan. You should include a statement of your business vision, or goals, and a profile of any business partners, including background and education that will lend to your success. You should honesty outline your competition and market, as well as describe your marketing plan and how the business will be financed. You are taking a snapshot of you ideas, background, the research and planning, and the hopes you have for your starting and running a successful business; be sure to word it in manner that anyone reading your business plan should take you, and your ideas, seriously.

The format of your business plan should include the following;

- A title page
- A table of contents
- An executive summary of the business you intend to start
- A general description of the business and the services offered
- A accurate market analysis of your competition
- A marketing plan
- A management profile describing how the business will be run and by whom
- A personal and business financial profile

Note: If you are purchasing an existing business, you can ask the seller if they are willing to share their business plan with you. This will give you a big head start on the process.

In short, your business plan should convey the Who, What, When, Where, Why, and How of your business from start-up, financing, operation, marketing, management, and onto the near future where it will be profitable. Your business plan should show what you are planning is a good investment for a bank, even if you are not using one, and more importantly, for you and your future.

Now go get a book on writing business plans and put some hard effort into it. The result will show that you are willing and able to start, run, and manage a successful business.

CHAPTER 10

Polices and Procedures

The policies and procedures you implement in running your inn will be as unique as you are. In many ways, policies and procedures create the personality, or feel of your inn, and will greatly impact your guests' experience, and the manner in which you operate your business. As unique as your operating procedures may be, there are still some common issues for you to consider. Let's talk about a few.

Reservation Procedures

You will avoid a lot of stress if you adopt clear-cut reservation procedures and a firm cancellation policy. When taking reservations, you should have a form that includes all the information you need to obtain. At minimum you will need to collect the same information you would provide if you were making a reservation at a hotel for a vacation. Name, address, telephone numbers, number of guests, arrival and departure dates, and a credit card number to secure the reservation are all necessary. Beyond this information, you may also want to obtain an email address to send out a confirmation and ask if there are any special dietary, mobility, or allergy considerations.

You have a few options when accepting and tracking guest data from a pencil and paper ledger to more sophisticated and expensive guest-tracking software. If you are familiar with office management and have used them in the past, you can get by very well using Microsoft Access and Excel to keep your guest records. In our case, we capture the initial data on a guest reservation form and once a guest checks in we transfer it to a database.

On our reservation form Michelle has included a notes section where she records any special requirements a guest may have such as requesting that a blow dryer or ironing board and iron be available. Following their stay, she also records any pertinent information we may have learned by their visit such as how they like their eggs, if they want espresso instead of regular coffee, or if they like their room warm or cool. This way we can tailor our preparations on their next stay. Guests notice this, and feel very welcome for your efforts. In one case, we had a guest that was allergic to eggs but loved the smell of Michelle's fresh baking. Now when she comes for a visit, Michelle always bakes a special treat using egg substitute. I cannot tell you how appreciative our guest is for this caring special treatment.

Remember, being an innkeeper is first and foremost about the relationships you build with your guests. You will get to know them and even develop friendships with your regulars. Just as you would do for a friend, you will have a desire to treat them as special. This will keep your guest coming back as well as build a positive reputation of your inn and enrich all parties involved.

The first time Michelle and I learned we had a "reputation" was very surprising. A couple staying with us visited a classy restaurant in our area, and over the course of their meal mentioned to the restaurant owner that they were staying at our inn. Both the owner and their server commented that they have heard good things about us and that they would recommend to anyone that they stay with us. We were very flattered to say the least, but if you think about it, this was our intention all along. In everything we did, from decorating to customer service, we intended our guests to have an enjoyable stay, and apparently our efforts have paid off.

Payment Policy

When to charge your guests for their stay is also a consideration. I know innkeepers who actually charge a customer in full at the time they make their reservation. Others wait until the guest checks in to charge them. In our case, we wait to run their credit card until they check out. This allows our guests the ability to purchase something from the gift corner and include the cost, or use another form of payment, such as an alternate credit card or cash.

Note: If you will accept personal checks, state any additional requirements such as two forms of ID clearly in your policies. Most innkeepers we know will only accept personal checks for advance payment, ensuring the check has time to clear before the guest's arrival. You may also be comfortable accepting checks from repeat guests with whom you are familiar.

However you chose to handle payment, you should consider some of the pitfalls. Most credit card processing companies will charge you a higher processing fee if you key-in the card info as opposed to swiping the actual card, as you would if the guest was standing there. There are also fees if you charge a deposit early and then complete the transaction for the entire amount at a later date. When taking cash, you may be tempted to keep the income off the books. I do not recommend you do so. Give to Caesar what belongs to Caesar and keep your records accurate and your taxes paid. This is important for obvious legal reasons, and can have an impact if you apply for business loans or disclose your income when you sell your business. See what other innkeepers in your area do and develop a policy that is comfortable for you.

In one case, we had a guest that checked in for a one-night stay to attend an event nearby, and she asked to pay her bill at check-in, as she was leaving early the next morning. Luckily, she did this, as she was surprised to find an old flame at the event with which she had a bad breakup. She stormed out and came back to the inn quite upset. She quickly gathered her belongings and left in a hurry, not staying overnight. I was glad she had already paid, as I would not have wanted to be the one who stopped her in the parking lot to insist on payment!

Cancellation Policy

Having a clearly stated cancellation policy is also important. Your policy should be fair but firm, and clearly listed on your web site and confirmation documents that you send or email to your guests. If you have trouble with conflict, it will be difficult for you when a guest cancels their reservation and you have to charge them a rebooking fee, or even the full rate, depending on timing and your policies. Many guests understand, but most will try to avoid paying altogether, as they feel they've received nothing for their money. Having provided them with a clear cancellation policy on their confirmation document is your best defense in these circumstances.

Keep in mind that renting rooms is what you do for a living. If you went to the place of business of one of your guests and asked them to provide their service or product for free most would laugh, so don't feel bad about following your policy. In many cases, you will have turned away another potential guest because of a reservation already being on the books, a reservation that would have generated income for you. If you like, you can offer a canceling guest a discount on a future stay or a credit for future use. For our regulars who we must charge because of an unexpected cancellation, we may extend a 50% discount on a future night, or one night free with a multi-night stay in the future.

Note: Something we were told by our fellow innkeepers that proved to be true is the abundance of family deaths that occur when a guest cancels a reservation. This can be a difficult situation if someone is truly grieving, but in many cases, this is simply an excuse that lets them off the hook gracefully. The question is; how can you be sure the guest has truly suffered a loss? The answer is—you can't. Again, a firm cancellation policy is your best defense. This happens so often that we have included a disclaimer on our cancellation policy that clearly states the policy applies even in the case of bereavement.

> *Michelle's Thought: Legitimate bereavement cancellations, unfortunately, do occur, so always err on the side of a real demise. In these genuine cases, the last thing a guest will be thinking or will be worried about will be whether or not you charge their credit card for your loss of business. Be polite, sympathetic, and professional. At least your guests were kind enough to call and cancel, not leaving you to expect them.*

Most inns post their cancellation policy on their web sites. Instead of reinventing the wheel, you can research what other innkeepers in your area are doing and customize a cancellation policy that works for you. Here is an example:

CANCELLATIONS

There is a 14-day cancellation policy. Cancellations made at least 14 days in advance of your scheduled arrival will result in a full refund, less a 10% bookkeeping charge. If you cancel your reservation within 14 days of your scheduled arrival, then the full amount of your deposit (50% of your charge) will be forfeited. If you must cancel within 48 hours of scheduled arrival, your entire room rate will be charged. If we are able to re-book the room after your cancellation, you will be issued a credit voucher good for a stay with us for anytime within one year.* (*some scheduling restrictions apply.)

Children and Pets

Allowing children and pets is a decision you should consider carefully. While opening your doors to more potential guests can generate more income, it can also drive guests away. This is where knowing your market becomes important. If your inn is near family attractions, you may hurt yourself by disallowing children. If most of your guests come for a peaceful retreat, having noisy children running through your inn may put them off. In the case of pets, you may have guests who are allergic to pet dander and will be distressed to find pets, or even to find that you have previously allowed pets in the rooms.

Your children and pets policies should be clear. In our case, we have no restrictions on children over the age of twelve, but require at least one adult for each child under the age twelve. This policy grew out of experience. In one case we had a single mother who came for the weekend bringing her two five-year old children, and unexpectedly, a friend's young son. This did not stop her from taking her relaxation time however, as she went outside to enjoy the weather and read a book on the porch. The problem was, she left the kids to run free in the inn and I guess, assumed Michelle and I would watch after them. Luckily they were the only guests that weekend and we survived the imposition.

Many of your guests will be retired couples whose children are grown and they now travel with their pets instead, and allowing them can enhance your business. Beyond the concerns for other guests who may be allergic, you should also consider what your policy would be should a guest's pet soil the carpet in a room or even be unfriendly to other guests. In our case, we do allow pets under twenty pounds, but we require that guests with pets stay in our suite, which has a private entrance with easy access to the outside, and offers some sound insulation from the other guest rooms should their pet make noise. Most pet-accompanied guests understand this policy, and are very grateful that we will accommodate them at all. It is nice for us too, as we in turn rent out or highest-rate room.

Note: Ironically, we have found pets far less of a problem than young children. For some reason, many parents do not feel the need to monitor their children's behavior in a home-like bed & breakfast environment, but most travel-along pets are used to traveling, and are extremely well behaved.

Smoking

Smoking is a sensitive subject; quite simply, the best way to go is to not allow smoking inside your inn. So many folks are put off by the smell that you will definitely drive away guests if you allow it. Smoking also presents a fire danger, and may have an impact on your insurance rates. We do allow smoking outside, but state clearly in our policy that it is not allowed within forty feet of any door. Most smokers are used to some restrictions and are not offended by such a policy. If you are going to provide exterior smoking areas, be sure to also provide receptacles for cigarette butts, or you will find them on the ground, something that may put off your non-smoking guests.

Check-in and Check-out Times

When guests can expect to check-in and checkout should be clearly posted in your rooms. Some states require that a card indicating the minimum and maximum room rates and the check-in and checkout times, along with fire evacuation procedures, be posted clearly in each guest room. Even if it is not mandated, it is wise to do so.

We allow check-in anytime after 3:00 PM and checkout is at 11:00 AM. Remember the reservation sheet? If a guest asks for early check-in or late checkout we will accommodate them if possible, but there is a $15.00 charge. Keep in mind that if you are going from one full night to another you will need the time between 11:00 and 3:00 to turn your rooms and clean the inn, so offering early or late arrival and departure may not be possible. In most cases, you will be able to accommodate such a request.

Note: We include early check-in and late checkout with rental of our suite and we usually do not charge our regulars for this service. We will also temporarily store luggage for guests who require such service.

Minimum Stay

Your minimum stay policy can be a source of great anxiety if you are not clear or consistent about it. Some innkeepers require a two-night minimum on weekends (Friday and Saturday nights), others have minimum stay requirements and modified rates based on the season, and others always require more than one night. You should see what other inns in your market are doing and consider adopting similar policies. This will breed good will between you and other innkeepers and prevent potential guests from getting different answers on minimum stay requirements from neighboring inns.

In our first year in business, I was very hesitant turning away any business at all, and we did not mandate a minimum stay. Our neighboring innkeepers encouraged us to adopt the same stay policy as they implemented, and cautioned that if we took numerous one-night reservations we would lose far more multi-night guests. Well, this was exactly the case. When we took the weekend one-nighters, we found that more often than not we ended up turning away guests asking for the entire weekend. Further, we became known for taking one-night reservations and were bombarded with this type of guest. When we finally adopted the same two-night policies as our fellow innkeepers, our business actually increased, and our guest quality also improved.

Note: You are running a bed and breakfast, not a hotel. The type of guest who patronizes a B&B expects a higher level of accommodation and service, and understands that the premise of a B&B is built around longer stays. Single-night guests are usually those that cannot find a cheaper accommodation close by and are predisposed to feeling that they are paying too much for an overnight stay. These guests tend to be more demanding, less satisfied, and will usually not return, no matter how pleasant you try to make their stay.

All this being said, you will have to take one-night stay requests on a case-by-case basis. For the most part, taking a mid-week one-night stay is fine. You may also accommodate returning guests with a single night stay in anticipation of future multi-night reservations. There are also slow times where renting any room is welcome and requiring a two-night minimum would be foolish. You will learn what is right for you and your business through much trial and error.

Michelle's Thought: With minimum stay, as well as other policies, it can be difficult to remain consistent. There ARE exceptions to every rule...but rules mean nothing if you don't stick to them more often than you bend or break them. Whenever a potential guest tries to argue a policy, I try looking at it as being fair to ALL our guests to simply stay with the rules. With minimum stay, we created a 14-day window before an event in which we WILL take a one-night reservation on a weekend, and we give our guests the option of calling back within that window instead. It's not a guarantee of an available room, but is an alternative to turning down a potential guest completely, and might give you the chance to fill an empty room for at least one night on a weekend that didn't fill up.

Single Groups

Consideration should be given to your policy of renting all the rooms in your inn to a single group. Many innkeepers have found that filling your inn with a single group your guests will tend to be more boisterous, less courteous of your belongings, and make bigger messes. You may find having at least one room rented to a stranger to the group will curb such behavior. If you adopt such a policy, you may waive this requirement for wedding groups, seniors, tour groups, or others you are comfortable with.

Refusing Business

Plain and simple, you have the right to refuse service to anyone. Now, this may seem contrary to your desire to put heads in your beds to make money, but there are times you may exercise this right. If a potential guest is drunk, shows up with a sheep, refuses to provide payment or ID, or a myriad of other scenarios that may be uncomfortable to you, you may refuse to allow them to stay with you. Remember, it is your home too, and you should be comfortable with whom you allow inside.

Note: Although Michelle and I have so far avoided the nightmare of having to turn away a guest at the door, we have refused to take reservations over the phone. It has been our experience that if a potential guest calls and immediately wants a discount on the room rate, or asks to avoid minimum stay requirements, they will arrive already dissatisfied, mostly because they already feel they are paying too much, or being robbed of their hard earned cash by paying for two nights when they only needed one. In these cases, we try to discourage, or even refuse, having them stay with us. Negative emotions can be contagious to your other guests and compromise positive word of mouth advertising. In some cases it is better to have an empty bed than a grumpy guest.

Operational Concerns

The procedures for running your inn will develop over time as you become more comfortable as an innkeeper. There are a couple of major items you will need to consider immediately. One is how often you will change guest sheets and towels, and the other is breakfast.

You should always give your guests the option of having fresh sheets and towels every day if they desire. A door card that says "Do Not Disturb" on one side, and "Ready to Clean" on the other may be enough. In our case, we advise guests that we change their sheets after two days use unless otherwise requested, and ask them to place towels they want changed on the floor while hanging those they will use again on the rack.

In many cases, we have guests who ask us not to change their sheets for their entire stay. Others want fresh towels daily, and we are happy to accommodate them. The way we look at it is; they are paying the same rate each day and if they want all their linens fresh, they are certainly entitled. Most guests in this day and age are environmentally conscious and will reuse their linens willingly.

Note: Remember what is important to a bed and breakfast; a clean, comfortable bed, quality towels and bed linens, and a satisfying breakfast.

Providing your guests with a satisfying breakfast is very important to their impression of your inn and their overall satisfaction with their stay. When we started out, Michelle and I adopted a policy of offering deluxe continental style breakfast midweek and a full, cooked breakfast on weekends. What we have discovered is that flexibility is the key. Many mid-week guests are business type travelers and are happy setting their own schedule and serving themselves from our continental bar. Others who are on vacation expect the full B&B treatment and look forward to a home-cooked breakfast.

Whatever you decide is right for you make sure your guests know in advance what to expect. We include our breakfast policy on our web site so there are no surprises, but we usually decide on making a full breakfast based on our guests' needs. Some weekend guests are light eaters and are happy with the continental bar, and some mid-weekers would be unhappy if we did not make Michelle's famous soufflé.

Note: It has been our experience that offering your guests choices adds greatly to their feeling of enjoyment. Our continental bar has fresh fruit, cereal, fresh breads, yogurt, two kinds of juice, pastries, and of course, coffee and tea. When we cook, we always offer at least two choices, such as stuffed strawberry French toast or soufflé, or fresh-picked- blueberry pancakes or eggs to order.

Even if your guests never touch your fresh-baked muffins or only have coffee for breakfast, they will enjoy seeing the choices you have set out for them, and remember that they felt as if they could always have had more. Having you guests feel satisfied is your goal, and with any luck, will cause them to speak well of you and recommend your inn to others.

Michelle's Thought: Give your guests the chance to decide how much interaction they'd like to have with you. Give them their space, but be approachable and linger nearby should they need anything. Try to feel each group and person out individually, and though you may be interested in a guest's destination, background, or family, remember, they may be tired from traveling, and lots of questions might overwhelm them or seem intrusive.

Feedback

In order to fine-tune your operational procedures, it is important to get feedback from your guests. This can be accomplished by first observing them. If they seem happy, they probably are. If you are comfortable doing so, you may ask them directly if they would change anything about their experience. Be prepared to hear anything, and accept critique with a smile or you may ruin your chances of them booking a return stay. A nice way of getting feedback that does not make you or your guests uncomfortable is to provide feedback cards. Guests can anonymously write down their concerns and you get business improvement advice from your most important source, your customers.

CHAPTER 11

Energy Management

With today's rising energy costs, a brief discussion on energy management is warranted. After your mortgage, energy costs; electric, gas, fuel oil, and water will be your largest business expense and anything you can do to limit these costs will reflect positively on your bottom line.

There is no magic here, the less you use of these utilities, the lower your expense. Finding ways to reduce usage can be as easy as conducting a home energy audit of your property. Most local power companies offer guides on what to look for, and simple, cost- effective repairs you can make to reduce your energy usage. Beyond these recommendations, there are a few things as a B&B owner to consider.

Guests will not want to compromise feeling warm in the winter or cool in the summer. If you can control the temperature of your rooms individually, that is best. It allows you to only heat or cool the rooms that are occupied and conserve energy on those that are not. If you have a common thermostat, you will have to let your guests' comfort dictate the temperature that is best for them. You can, however, turn down the heat, or set the AC temperature higher when the space is not in use to reduce power and fuel usage.

Electricity usage is another area you can greatly reduce with some small changes. First and foremost I recommend changing ALL of your light bulbs to compact fluorescents. These bulbs can now be purchased in soft white, giving the same warm glow of conventional bulbs, and they are cost-effective due to their long life.

Note: Including our lamps and exterior fixtures, we swapped out over 75 bulbs for compact fluorescents reducing our energy use from 7,500 watts to just under 1,200 for the same light output.

Another area to check for wasted electricity is your room television sets. Many TV's actually use more power when on standby, and can be costing you money even when not in use. An easy solution to this problem is use a switched power strip that you can turn off when your rooms are unoccupied.

If you provide nightlights in your guest areas or bathrooms you should consider the switched type over the automatic ones that come on by themselves when it gets dark. We have found that may guests unplug the unstitched ones anyway, as the ambient light disturbs their sleep.

Heating your hot water is another big user of energy. Most newer hot water heaters are fairly energy efficient if maintained properly. The main thing to check is the temperature setting on the tank. It should be high enough to allow ample hot water for multiple guests taking showers in succession, but low enough not to scald them. You should ensure that your heater could provide enough hot water for all of your guests to take a morning shower.

Note: If you are replacing or increasing the size of your hot water heater, a very important rating to know is its recovery time. A propane heater may be able to reheat 80 gallons of water in 20 minutes, where an electric one may take up to two hours.

The last area of usage you can control is your water use. The heaviest use will come from guest showering. Most new showerheads are rated at 2.5 gallons per minute of flow, older heads can flow twice as much. Even at 2.5 gpm if a guest takes a twenty-minute shower that equals fifty gallons of water use. While most showers are a mix of both hot and cold water, this does not mean that most of your hot water tank will become depleted, but it is still a large amount of water through your meter. For maximum efficiency, install showerheads with water flow rates of 2.5 gallons per minute, or gpm.

There are two types of low flow showerheads: aerating and laminar-flow. Aerating heads mix air with the water making a misty spray. Laminar-flow heads form individual streams of water making the shower spray feel more robust and create less steam. When renovating an inn built before 1992, you should check the flow of the current showerheads, as they could be as much as 5.5 gpm. To check your flow rates, you can place a one-gallon bucket under the head and time how long it takes to fill. If it fills in less than 20 seconds, you could benefit by installing a low-flow showerhead.

Remember, guest comfort should be your main priority. I have personally showered in every shower in our inn to feel the characteristics of each showerhead and ensure that our guests are going to be satisfied with their shower experience. Whenever I travel and stay at an inn or hotel, the quality and feel of the shower is something I definitely notice. If the water does not get hot enough, or the showerhead has poor pressure or flow, my satisfaction with my stay is severely diminished.

CHAPTER 12

Advertising and Promotion

Before we get into advertising your inn, lets talk about your inn's name. What's in a name? Everything! The name of your inn will become its identity, and to some degree, yours too. People will say, "There goes that couple who run the such-and-so inn." Also, the name of your inn may be telling of your best amenities like; "The Beach House Inn", or, "Mountain Top Bed & Breakfast." Whatever you chose it should be distinctive and work with your theme. Our Inn is called the "New England House Bed & Breakfast." This works for us as, we are in the center of New England and have 6 guest rooms, each themed after one of the six New England states.

In essence, choosing the name of your B&B is the first piece of advertising you will do and it should be given careful consideration to be descriptive of your uniqueness.

Promoting your Inn

Promoting your inn can be very challenging. You have numerous options for advertising your business from print to the web. Most innkeepers will tell you that in this day and age most of their business comes from the Internet. For this reason, you should first and foremost concentrate on your web page and Internet presence.

Internet Presence

There are numerous build-your-own web site services on the Internet and these can be a cost effective way for you to design and build your own web page. If you are not that adventurous you may want to hire a web designer. No matter which avenue you choose, here again you want to do your research. Visit as many B&B web sites as you can and take notes of the features you like. For instance, some B&B's incorporate music on their web pages, I personally find this distracting, but you may like the addition and want to build a similar feature into your web site.

Pictures of your inn, both outdoors and indoors, are important. Most digital cameras are of a fine enough quality that you can do this yourself. You should take numerous views of each guest room, common areas, and outside views that are inviting. You can also include pictures of a specialty breakfast dish you like to serve or picturesque views from guest room windows if you have them. Take as many pictures as you like, as you will be able to review them and choose the best ones to use on your site later.

Note: Most digital cameras take very high mega-pixel images that provide high quality prints and computer images, however, the higher the mega-pixels, the longer your pictures will take to load when a potential guest visits your web site. There is nothing more frustrating for an experienced web user than waiting for pictures to load. The best solution to this problem is to use software that is readily available on most freeware sites that will resize your pictures for web use without compromising quality.

When building your web page, be sure to include the basics, such as address and telephone numbers, as well as an email address as many folks will contact you that way. You should also include an inviting description of your inn, amenities that you offer, and reservation and cancellation policies. You may also want to add information about yourself and the history of your particular inn. Providing information and links about local points of interest and attractions is also helpful.

Whatever you do, do not scrimp on your web page. You can be economical by designing it yourself, but the finished product should be of very high quality as this is your "sign" in the cyber world and potential guests will make decisions on staying with you based heavily on the image you project. That being said, make sure the image you project is truly what a guest will see when they arrive, or you will likely disappoint them. If you change the layout or furnishings of a particular room, update your web site pictures to reflect the changes.

The best course of action when considering your web site is to talk to friends who have sites of their own in any area of business. They will provide you with a wealth of information, and share their mistakes; this will assist you greatly with the numerous decisions and choices you will have to make in designing your own site.

B&B Web Brokers

There are hundreds of sites that promote tourism and lodging throughout the United States and the world, and you will be solicited by all of them. Michelle and I promote our inn on about a dozen such sites like bbdirectory, inndirectory, bellhop.com and others. These sites usually list all of their member facilities by state and provide links to your site or forward reservation requests to you by email. These sites exist on the revenue generated by you subscribing to be listed on their directory and some can be quite expensive. Here again, it pays to do your research and determine which broker sites you want to be associated with. One suggestion is to see what sites your neighboring B&B's are listed on and consider using the same ones at first. People like to compare, and if your inn is listed next to those of your competition, you will get more "hits" or visits to your site. The more hits you get, the more reservations you will realize.

Note: You should establish a monthly budget for advertising and stick to it. You can easily overspend on advertising when you are starting up and attempting to determine what media is best for you. Trial and error will be the guiding factor at first. Monitor your advertising results by asking all of your inquires how they heard of you and keep track of this information so you can target your advertising dollars on what works. You may also want to install a hit-tracker that tells you in report format where your Internet inquiries originated and if there have been multiple hits from the same source. This can be helpful in determining if the broker sites are actually driving business to you.

Print Media

It has been our experience that the best bang for your buck when using print media is to advertise locally and regionally. Small town papers, local shopper's guides, and annual stay-and-play type guides are best. If you have special local-only offerings such as banquet or wedding facilities, these too are best advertised in demographically appropriate print media.

Another print medium that is a very good value is to join your local chamber of commerce that will include you in their business directory and special advertising. Seasoned travelers will often check with the local COC to see if they have any recommendations for lodging or have had any complaints about your business. Being listed as a business in good standing with your local chamber is a wise investment.

One last suggestion for print advertising is to join a local B&B association or regional tourism promotion group that combines the limited financial resources of member businesses and advertises in a larger medium that you may not be able to afford individually. Many of these groups print rack cards for distribution at information centers and rest stops, or even advertise in foreign tourism brochures and mailers. There are additional benefits from belonging to local associations such as networking with other innkeepers.

One print medium you will not want to skimp on is your street sign. It is the first impression potential guests will have of your inn. You should make it a good one!

Again, you can spend, spend, and spend, on print media and the only way you will know if it is working is to ask your guests how they found you. If they say they saw your ad in the local shopper, you will certainly want to continue your advertising in that publication.

Radio and Television

Most inns, especially start-ups, will not have the budget for radio or television advertising. You may want to splurge when you first open to let folks know you are there by using these sources in a limited way. Most cable providers can target TV spots to certain areas to reduce costs, and short "tags" at the end of larger advertiser spots on the radio can also be reasonable in cost. If you are clever, you may even be able to get coverage for free by sending out a press release to your local TV and radio stations advising them of your grand opening or public open house. If you have anything unique to your inn, such as incorporating numerous alternative energy sources in your renovation, they may also be interested in producing a story on that angle. You simply do not know unless you try.

When Michelle and I opened our inn, it had been a vacant home in a very visible part of town for quite some time. We knew we were generating quite a bit of interest from local townsfolk, as we would see them driving by to see our renovation progress and overheard comments when visiting the town general store. When we finished with our renovations, but prior to opening for business, we advertised on the local cable channel that we were having an open house for folks to see all we had done. It was a great success, and not only satisfied the curiosity of our neighbors, it allowed us to meet them face to face and get to know them better. I am not certain that it is completely due to these meetings, but we now receive almost 20% of our business from local residents who send visiting family and friends our way.

Brochures

You will absolutely want to develop and print a nice brochure for your inn. Folks who lodge with you will take them to show others where they stayed. If you offer banquet facilities or wedding accommodations, clients might take them to mail with their invitations. We put brochures in our lobby, and are always having to replenish the supply.

Brochures should include all the same information as your web site, just a bit more briefly, as well as listing your web address. The most popular format is an 8 ½ by 11 tri-fold brochures that includes pictures. I have seen these in monochromatic format, but full-color ones are far more inviting. If you are on a budget, most better-quality office printers can produce quality printing and picture reproduction saving the cost of a professional.

A Gimmick

When considering advertising, gimmicks can be attention grabbers, you know, "free with every purchase" or "today only". Gimmicks can work for inns too, if you have one. Your device can be as simple as promoting your location, "private beach", "nearby many attractions", or "close to skiing!" You may offer services that set you apart, such as spa facilities or bicycle tours, whatever makes you unique can be your gimmick. Many inns have built their entire clientele solely on some unique product, service, or attraction they can boast they offer that their competitors do not. If you cater to hunters, race fans, golfers, quilters, scrap bookers, whatever suits you, say it loud and proud on all of your media. Who knows, if you offer free foot massages with every room rental, you may become the favorite destination for hikers visiting your area.

The bottom line is the old adage "it pays to advertise" is true; it is simply your task to determine where and how you will do so. This is something that sounds simple, but will continually be a part of running a successful bed and breakfast.

CONCLUSION

Owning and operating your own Bed and Breakfast can be a fulfilling way to make a living. Remember, being an innkeeper is a lifestyle that will require you to look at work differently than if you work in a traditional office setting. Your home is your office, and your customers will be present at times you usually consider your own time. Guests will unknowingly test your patience and intrude on your privacy. You may just be sitting down to dinner, and someone will ask for more towels or directions to a local restaurant. Understanding the change in your lifestyle ahead of time will help you service your guests with a gracious demeanor.

When building your business plan, be sure to include time for yourself. You should consider what your office hours will be, and after what time, perhaps you won't answer the phone. You should allow for a vacation each year, getting away and letting someone pamper you for a change can recharge you for another year. If you are sharing innkeeper duties with a spouse or partner, you should clearly define responsibilities such as cooking, bookkeeping, housekeeping, maintenance, and all the other aspects associated with running a B&B.

Remember that you are your own employer and you will need to provide things like your own medical insurance, and you can't just call out sick to get a day off. You should plan for what you are going to do after inn keeping, and set-up a 401K or other personal retirement or investment plan. If you have employees, you may need to provide like benefits to them, which can be a daunting task. You will be responsible for paying and filing business and income taxes, as well as all required record keeping. If something breaks, you must immediately fix it, or hire someone to do it for you. You are the boss and the buck stops with you. You should be prepared for this responsibility.

Once you develop a routine, you will find that being an innkeeper will provide you many rewards as well. You will have greater control of your schedule. When you get up in the morning, you will already be at work and won't have to commute through traffic. If you want to take time in the middle of the day to attend your son's soccer game, you can easily do so. You can wear clothes that are comfortable to you, you can enjoy your hobbies more fully, perhaps even taking time to write a book about it! But mostly, you will feel the freedom and satisfaction that comes with being the master of your own destiny and having more control of your own time and life.

Michelle and I wish you all the greatest success in opening and running your own bed and breakfast. Thank you for letting us share our experiences with you and, Happy Innkeeping!

Hindsight is 20/20

Planning

- Do your homework.
- Apprentice at an inn if possible. Stay at as many as you can and observe.
- Have a 12-month reserve of projected operating expenses.

- Visit with all regulatory agencies and officials in advance.
- Stay at a B&B in the location you intend to open one and be a tourist.

Renovations

- Each room needs its own bathroom.
- Soundproof the walls.
- Place at least one electrical outlet on every wall.
- Repair or replace any window that does not operate properly.
- Make at least one room ADA accessible.

Operations

- Don't reinvent the wheel. Ask others how they do it and why.
- Hire professionals where you need the help, such as web design or accounting.
- Define the duties of each partner and employee, including shifts.
- Don't automatically discount your rates or compromise policies at guest request.
- Always ask for the CV code when taking a credit card number.

Policies

- Conform to what other inns in the area do at first.
- Consider if you want to allow children. The same goes for pets.
- Develop a fair but firm minimum-stay and cancellation policy and stick to it.
- Don't easily discount your rates.
- Have office and non-office hours.

Industry Trends

The information provided here is a compilation from numerous industry sources and not specific to any particular group or survey. We encourage you to take some time and do your own research on industry trends for Bed & Breakfast's specific to your geographic location and intended market.

- The average bed and breakfast guest is 20 to 49 years old.
- Typical B&B guests are well educated, have professional backgrounds, and are in the upper income percentile.
- The typical booking is for two guests.
- Location of the B&B and availability are the most important features.
- Allowing pets and smoking are least important.
- Most B&B guests are traveling for pleasure.
- The most important amenity feature is mattress quality, followed by towels and linens.
- Comfort items like drinking glasses, bath mats, reading lights, and soaps are also important.
- Mints on the pillow, shampoo and conditioner, and in-room phones are less important.
- Guests enjoy space to set toiletries, a comfortable chair with a reading lamp, a lighted mirror, bedside tables, luggage racks, clothes hangers, extra pillows, and ample hot water; all are highly commented on.
- Repeated comments mention comfortable beds and adequate lighting as important.
- Today's health-conscious guests enjoy the quiet solitude of private baths.
- Quality items such as the warmth of the innkeeper, having a private bath, and a good breakfast are most important to B&B guests.
- Other important quality items are privacy, gardens, cleanliness, charm, and décor.
- In general, the older the inn, or more history-associated, the higher room rates.
- In addition to basic room rates, guests will pay a premium for fireplaces, whirlpool tubs, and a balcony or deck.

Note: Lodging industry statistics show that the Bed and Breakfast industry is healthy and enjoys strong annual increases in occupancy rates and revenues, even as hotel and motel bookings decline. Keep in mind that B&B guests are usually of a higher income level and thus more economically insulated from the downturns that effect hotel and motel traffic. They are also willing to pay for high-quality service, comfort, luxury amenities, and the other extras associated with staying at a B&B.

Sources: BedandBreakfast.com, PAII Bed and Breakfast and Country Inn Surveys, Inngoers Amenities Survey, The Professional Association of Innkeepers, Insider Magazine survey, Bed and Breakfast Industry Survey Analysis, Market Analysis of Bed and breakfast Guides, Economic Review of Travel in the US.

ABOUT THE AUTHORS

Michelle and Chris started a bed and breakfast simply to be able to spend every day together. Having a very close and loving relationship themselves, they love to welcome other people into their home, and entertain joyfully. Their combined strengths, talents, and experiences contributed to them becoming fun and efficient Innkeepers, a livelihood and lifestyle that suit them well. Married in an intimate beach ceremony in the Cayman Islands in June 2003, friends and family all comment on the compatibility of the couple, and see their obvious happiness in their time spent together. All agree, Chris and Michelle should be together in all they do. They now run the New England House Bed & Breakfast in Andover, New Hampshire.

Michelle graduated the Maryland Institute College of Art with a degree in Art Education. She lived and worked in Andover most of her young life, attended Andover Elementary/Middle School, and worked in a country store off Main Street as a teenager. Most of her large family still lives in the immediate area.

Chris holds degrees in Fire Science, Emergency Medicine, and Mass Communications. After a successful twenty-five year career in the fire service as a Nationally Registered Paramedic, Fire Marshal, and Assistant Fire Chief, he is now enjoying semi-retirement. Chris spent his early years in rural Pennsylvania, and later moved to Florida, where he resided for over 30 years before returning with Michelle to New Hampshire.

Chris and Michelle's dream to have a business they can pursue together has come true, and their hope is that by sharing their experience in opening the New England House Bed & Breakfast, others will be motivated to take the leap into the rewarding life of inn keeping.

If you would like to visit the New England House Bed & Breakfast, or simply email us with a question or comment, our web site is *www.nehbb.com.*

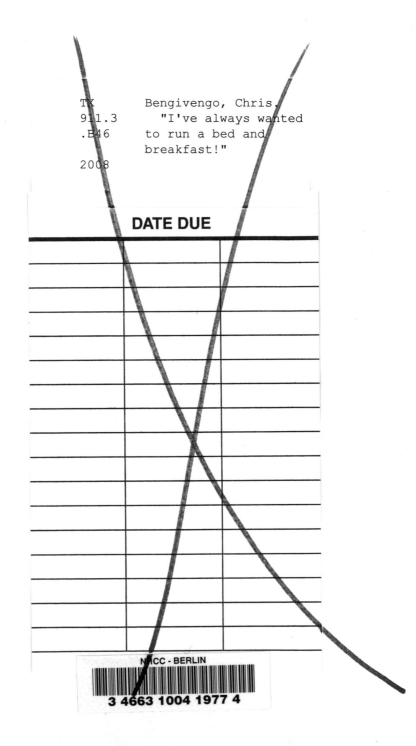

TX   Bengivengo, Chris,
911.3   "I've always wanted
.B46   to run a bed and
          breakfast!"

2008

DATE DUE